the last barrier

reshad feild

the last barrier

illustrated by salik chalom

harper & row, publishers
new york, hagerstown, san francisco, london

Portions of this book have appeared in "New Age Journal."

For information address Harper & Row, Publishers, Inc., 10 East 53rd Street, New York, N.Y. 10022. Published simultaneously in Canada by Fitzhenry & Whiteside Limited, Toronto.

First HARPER & ROW PAPERBACK edition published in 1977.

Designed by C. Linda Dingler

Library of Congress Cataloging in Publication Data

Feild, Reshad T.
The last barrier.
1. Sufism. 2. Feild, Reshad T. I. Title.
BP189.6.F44 1976 297'.4'0924 [B] 75-9345
ISBN 0-06-062586-4

85 86 10 9

This book is dedicated to Jessie Wood, my friend and editor, and to my beloved wife, Enisa, both of whom have helped make it possible for the book to come into print. And it is dedicated to the man I call "Hamid," without whose wisdom and guidance I would have nothing to say. So be it!

Come, come whoever you are,
Wanderer, worshipper, lover of leaving,
It doesn't matter.
Ours is not a caravan of despair.
Come, even if you have broken your vow
a thousand times.
Come, come yet again, come.
—Mevlana Jelalu'ddin Rumi

the last barrier

one

Whoever has heard of me, let him prepare to come and see me; whoever desires me, let him search for me. He will find me—then let him choose none other than I.

—Shams-i Tabriz

He who knows not, and knows not that he know not,
is a fool—shun him.
He who knows not, and knows that he knows not,
is a child—teach him.
He who knows, and knows not that he knows,
is asleep—wake him.
But he who knows, and knows that he knows,
is a wise man—follow him.

—Proverb

One autumn day as I was making my rounds of London's antique stores, I came upon a shop that was new to me. As an antique dealer I would visit a series of shops nearly every day, looking for special articles that I could buy cheaply and then resell at a greater price later on. On that particular day I felt drawn into a small shop tucked away in a back-street, which sold a variety of antiques, mainly from the Middle East. There was incense burning; the shop was quite dark, and as I walked in I immediately became aware of the powerful presence of the man who stepped forward to greet me. My first impression was of size. He was tall, well over six feet, heavily built, and was, I remember, wearing a blue suit. He had a mustache, wore glasses, and appeared to be in his early fifties.

"May I help you?" he asked.

"I would just like to look around if I may," I said, by now acutely aware of the tremendous presence, or power, that seemed to fill the shop.

Smiling, he said, "I am guessing that you are a dealer yourself, so don't take any notice of the prices marked on the tickets. Take your time." His voice was slightly accented and he was smoking a Turkish cigarette in a long holder.

My memory is hazy as to the exact sequence of events that then took place. All I know for certain is that some very deep instinct convinced me that this man knew something about a subject that had fascinated me for many years. As well as being an antique dealer I was also very involved with healing, as I had been cured by a healer of a serious illness some time before and had then discovered that I, too, had the gift of healing. All my spare time was taken up with treating people whom the orthodox medical profession had given up, either saying that their illnesses were simply psychosomatic, or else terminal, so that there was no more that could be done for them scientifically. While I practiced certain systems of healing I continually searched for more knowledge on the subject. During my research I had read a lot about the Dervishes of the Middle East, those extraordinary men who had given their lives totally to God and as such were reputed to have many miraculous powers. The more that I read about them, the more my interest had deepened. The study of the "way," which the Dervishes and the Sufis followed, became almost an obsession in my life, and yet, up to that moment, I had not met anyone who personally knew anything of the methods they used for healing or the various spiritual practices they followed. But there in that tiny antique shop I felt sure that I had come upon a key which would unlock a door into some of their secrets. Taking a deep breath I turned to face the shop keeper.

"You may think I'm crazy," I began, "and please forgive

me if I am asking the wrong question, but do you know anything about the Dervishes of the Middle East?"

The atmosphere in the shop seemed to change very suddenly. The man appeared taken aback, but recovering his composure carefully, he stubbed out his cigarette in an ashtray on the desk in front of him and then, after what seemed like an interminable length of time, he looked up.

"What an extraordinary question," he said, "Why do you ask?"

"I can only say that some sort of instinct prompted me to," I replied. "I have been studying books about their ways for a long time, and have been looking for someone who had some first-hand knowledge. For some reason it just occurred to me that perhaps you yourself came from the Middle East and might know something about them."

"And why should you think that, I wonder?" he asked very suspiciously.

Now that the question had come out I began to feel very uncomfortable and wished that I had not broached the subject. It was such an extraordinary situation. There was I, a thirty-four-year-old English antique dealer, confronting this huge man about a subject that is esoteric, to say the least, when neither of us had ever met before.

"Please excuse me," I stammered. "You must think me very ill-mannered."

"Not at all," he replied. He was smiling now. "Nothing ever happens by chance does it? Strangely enough I, too, am very interested in the Dervishes." He stared piercingly at me over the top of his glasses. "It is also time to close and I have some time to spare. Why don't you come and have coffee with me and we can talk about these things a little."

I do not remember leaving the shop nor walking up the street to find a place to have coffee. The whole situation was having a very strange effect on me. I was experiencing a very deep fear for no reason that I could understand at the time, as though I were just entering a world that was entirely new to me; and although part of me wished that I were somewhere else, there was another part that was holding me in a situation that eventually was to change the whole course of my life.

After we sat down and had ordered coffee he introduced himself, telling me that his name was Hamid, that he originally came from Turkey, and that he had been living in England for about two and a half years. He skirted around the subject that so fascinated me but did give me some information about the Dervishes in Turkey. He told me that Ataturk, the first President, had banned them because their power, even in politics, had become too great. Hamid also indicated that there were still people in Turkey who knew of their ways. In fact, the conversation, although very light, became more a period of questioning than anything else. I felt as though I was being very carefully analyzed. I began to be more and more uncomfortable.

"But I am very curious to know how you came to be so interested in these things," he said at last as we stood up to leave the café. "Perhaps you would like to come and have dinner with me in my apartment tomorrow evening and then we can talk further. Do you mind what you eat?"

Rather apologetically I explained that I had been a vegetarian for some years, but that I did not want to put him to any trouble. "That's fine," he said. "In fact here is another coincidence. I have just written a book on vegetarian dishes of the Middle East, so I will prepare something special for you. Come round tomorrow evening at seven-thirty."

With that he turned and disappeared into the crowd. For a moment I stood looking down the street after him and then returned to my apartment, where I lived alone as my wife and I had separated some time before. I do not think that I slept more than a few hours that night. My mind was racing, trying to fit together all that had transpired that day.

During the next year I spent as much time as possible with Hamid. We would sit for hours in his shop and, little by little and so subtly, he introduced me into the way of the Sufis, those who follow the mystic path of Islam. I became his pupil, avidly collecting as much information as I could, but for some reason I did not understand he would not talk to me about the particular subject that most fascinated me, namely the healing arts. When questioned about it he would just skirt around the subject, saying that he was sure that I was a sensitive and therefore would know what to do at the right time, and that was enough for then. "Keep to the straight way," he would say. "Do not get deviated. Always question your motive for pursuing these subjects. It is a dangerous game and it is necessary that you have a good foundation of real knowledge; otherwise you might get blown over."

About once a week I would go to his apartment for dinner. If he was still preparing the meal when I arrived, he would insist that I sit in silence until he had finished. He always worked with such concentration, and arranged the food so beautifully, that it was as though each meal was the most important he had ever cooked. He never questioned me about being a vegetarian until one day he looked up from the salad that he was arranging and asked, "Why are you a vegetarian?" I went into a long discourse about the merits of vegetarianism and its relation to the spiritual life until finally he interrupted me. "Good," he said. "But I am not a vegetarian. Do you know why?"

I shook my head.

He smiled. "I am not a vegetarian because I know that God is perfect, and therefore everything has its place in the universe. I am not criticizing you," he added, "but the further you proceed along the path, the more you must be able to transmute everything that comes your way. One day we will talk further about this."

That year passed quickly. Our relationship grew in depth, and it was not long before Hamid attended all the various lectures I was giving at that time. Mostly I gave talks on healing and what is called the "subtle" body of man, which can be seen or felt by those who have sufficiently developed their sensitivity. At that time the world was waking up to the possibility of a new way of life, and discussions of related subjects drew large crowds, particularly young people. Besides the lectures and giving weekend workshops, I was involved with a group studying various forms of meditation, from the East and the West, which could be used in psychotherapy, and the group had grown very large. Hamid would come to the meetings, and always in the same way. He would arrive just before I started, then leave just before the end so that no one might notice him. He asked that our relationship be kept quiet for the time being. The following day he would go over the events of the previous evening in great detail. Although he had said that he knew nothing about healing, it was becoming increasingly apparent from his remarks that he knew much more than he was prepared to talk about.

Then an event occurred that changed the course of our relationship. One day I received a letter from an old school acquaintance, wondering if I might be able to help a close friend of his. This man and his wife had suffered severe problems for several years. The wife had been hospitalized for a time, and had finally left him. Since then he had suffered from appalling spells of depression, verging on suicide, and would often lock himself into his room for days on end. Neither his doctors nor the other types of healers he had consulted had been able to help him.

I had never had such a case before, and as I was having dinner with Hamid that evening I told him about it and showed him the letter. To my surprise he was very much interested, and said that he would like to meet the sick man.

"May I come with you?" he asked.

"Of course," I said, "but I don't know what on earth I'm going to do."

"If you like, I will help," he announced, pouring the coffee.

"You would what?" I said, startled.

He turned to me, smiling. "I said that I would help you if you like. I do know a little about these things, but until now the time has not been right to talk with you about them."

"In all this time why didn't you tell me you knew something about healing?" I asked, baffled.

"You were doing quite all right on your own. There was no need, and anyway I was interested in observing the way your mind was working. Now, if you like, we will meet here the day after tomorrow at eleven in the morning. I will shut the shop for the day, and perhaps you can also get the day off. Tonight you should contact the man and say that we will come, and that he must buy a fresh white egg."

"Hamid, I really don't understand. What do you want him to do?"

"He must buy a good white egg, and he must keep it with him continuously for twenty-four hours before we see him. He should hold it as much as possible, and at night he should put it beside his bed on a small table, as close to his head as he can without danger of breaking it. Is that quite clear? Don't worry, we won't hurt him! Now go and call him. You may do it from here if you like."

I wondered what the response of the man on the other end of the telephone would be, but to my surprise he had no reaction to my instructions. He said that he would get the egg the next day, and would look forward to seeing us. He also mentioned that at that particular moment he was better than he had been for a long time.

Two days later, when I arrived at Hamid's apartment, he was wearing his best suit, his hair was still wet from the shower, and he was holding an empty paper bag which he handed to me, with instructions to keep it for him.

"What's it for?" I asked.

"It's for the egg," he replied. "We will take it away with us when we leave."

"Will you tell me what you are going to do with it?" I asked.

"Wait and see," he said, getting into the car. We drove in silence across Hyde Park toward Hampstead where the man lived. As we drove through the center of London, past Kensington Gardens, the idea of this man sitting and waiting for us, holding an egg, struck me as so improbable that I began to chuckle.

"What's so funny?" Hamid asked. "Do you not want this man to be better?"

"Of course I do," I replied.

"Then be serious, for heaven's sake. This is a very difficult business."

We drove in silence the rest of the way. Our destination turned out to be a small but beautiful Regency house on a peaceful terrace high up on Hampstead hill. Hamid's mood was strange—I had never seen him like this before. His eyes were half closed, his lips moving quietly as though he were talking to himself, or perhaps praying.

As soon as I stopped the car he opened the door and got out. By the time I had locked the car and hurried after him he had already gone into the house. We were greeted by a man of slight build who introduced himself as Malcolm. With many nervous gestures he ushered us into the living room and offered tea, which Hamid accepted. As he left the room Hamid turned to me and said, "Well, where is it?"

I glanced around involuntarily. "Where is what, Hamid?"

He seemed suddenly angry. "You're the sensitive, you should know. Something is very wrong in this house. Go and find it."

"But Hamid," I protested, "I can't just go looking around the house without his permission."

"Do as I tell you. Go upstairs and find out what is wrong."

At that point I felt less uncomfortable about roaming uninvited through the house than about disobeying Hamid. I had no idea what I was looking for, but there had been so much force behind Hamid's order that I reached the top of the stairs before I had time to question what I was doing. Four closed doors faced me on the second floor. The first two were to bedrooms, then a bath. The fourth room, however, was different. It was a studio. In the dark I could just make out a large painting in the middle of the room. As I turned from drawing open the window curtains I felt a tremendous shock.

The painting on the easel was almost seven feet tall, but its narrowness gave the illusion of even greater height. It depicted an enormous horse's skull and backbone rising from a motionless expanse of water. The backbone seemed translucent, as though consumed by pale fire, while the skull was suffused from within by a lurid red glow. As I examined the painting I became aware of tiny flames licking in and out of the vertebrae and the jaw. The sense of macabre evil about the painting was overwhelming. I shut the door quietly and went quickly down the stairs. Tea had been brought and the two were talking to one another.

"You found the bathroom all right?" Hamid asked me.

"Yes," I said, not knowing how else to reply. Hamid turned to Malcolm and asked if he might have some brown sugar for his tea. As the man disappeared once more into the kitchen Hamid asked me, "Well, what was it?"

As carefully as I could I told him. He seemed pleased, or possibly relieved. "Thank you," he said. "Now we can proceed."

When Malcolm returned with the sugar, Hamid began immediately. "You have the egg my friend asked you to buy? Give it to me, please."

Malcolm brought out the egg carefully from his jacket pocket and handed it to Hamid. Momentarily, Hamid held it, weighing it carefully in his hands. Then, calling for a pen, he began to write all over the egg in Arabic. Not a word was spoken during this time. When the shell of the egg was completely covered, Hamid turned and looked sternly at Malcolm.

"You have made a very serious mistake," he began. "Through misuse of sexual energy you have exposed yourself to great evil. I am told that this is the third time that you have asked for help. Is that correct?"

"What do you mean?"

"I mean that twice before you have been to those who know about these things, but you did not obey their instructions and therefore you did not improve. Is this not so?"

Malcolm, looking very ashamed, explained that indeed it was true that on two occasions before he had been to healers,

but that they had asked him to do certain things which he felt he could not carry out.

"What did they do to help you?" Hamid asked.

"They gave me special herbs and teas, mainly," he replied.

"But did they not forbid you to eat red meat for forty days, and did they not tell you that you must not touch alcohol during that period?"

Malcolm looked stubborn and bewildered. "How did you know that?" he asked.

"It is in the egg," Hamid replied. "All information is in the egg, is it not? Now, since you have asked for help, will you accept my treatment unconditionally?"

Malcolm nodded. "Then get a towel and put it around your neck," Hamid said. "I am going to break this egg on your forehead."

A shocked silence followed. Neither Malcolm nor I moved for a few moments, and then Hamid once again ordered him to get a towel. When he returned, Malcolm seemed desolate and somehow smaller than when he had left the room. The atmosphere was so tense that even Hamid was trembling slightly, his forehead covered with fine beads of perspiration. "Before I do this," he said, "you must promise to burn the picture upstairs, and you must also promise not to eat meat for forty days and forty nights, and to drink no alcohol during that period. If you fail this time there will be no other chance. Is that quite clear?"

Malcolm nodded sadly. "But why burn the picture?" he asked. "It is the best painting I have ever done."

"It may be a good picture, but it does not come from good. My friend has already told me of it. You must excuse us. I sent him upstairs to find out the source of what I could feel in this house."

Hamid rose to his feet. I could see Malcolm with his head slightly bent and his eyes closed just beneath the level of Hamid's left elbow. For a moment I wished that I had never become involved with Hamid at all. Then Hamid took two steps forward, raised his hand containing the egg, and brought it down with great force onto Malcolm's forehead, the egg bursting just above his eyebrows. It seemed literally to explode. The yolk and the white bounced off his nose and landed in a dirty yellow heap on his lap.

"Give me the paper bag, please," Hamid ordered.

He took the bag in his left hand and carefully scraped the mess into it. Then, having examined Malcolm to see if there were any more pieces of shell sticking to him, he handed the paper bag to me. Finally, he took the towel from Malcolm, and with great tenderness carefully wiped his face.

"All right," he said, "it is done. I am sorry to have messed up your suit, but the cleaners will take care of it. Come on now, open your eyes."

Hamid was smiling and the whole feeling of the room had changed. There was a new lightness in the air, and I noticed the sun streaming through the window onto the sofa where we had been sitting.

"Now remember, do as you have been told, for you will not be given another chance. Come," he said, turning to me. "Bring the bag. We must go."

He told me to drive to the southern part of London, to where the Thames cuts its way through the city. He was in a very jovial mood, telling jokes about his early days in Turkey, as though nothing had happened. At last I asked him to explain.

"There is nothing to explain," he said. "It is too early for you to learn about these things yet. One day, though, if you wish, we may talk a little more."

"But the egg just seemed to explode," I said, "and then all the yolk and the white landed on that one place. It isn't logical."

Hamid roared with laughter. "I told you," he said, "that the egg contained all the secrets that we wished to know."

Still I was not satisfied. I had witnessed an incredibly powerful scene, but somehow the situation lacked resolution. I had been a professional healer for over five years, but I had never seen anything with the depth and power of what Hamid had done today. It was a difference not only of degree but of kind. Finally I asked him, "Is the man really cured? Will he regain his health now?"

Hamid glanced at me gravely. "That depends entirely on him," he said. "We have given him everything he needs to recover completely, but we cannot force him to accept it. All we can do now is to offer our prayers."

We parked the car by the Thames embankment. Hamid hurried across the pavement and I followed him as quickly as I could. He had the paper bag in his hand and as he threw it out over the water anyone passing by would have thought that he was feeding the seagulls. He silently watched the bag sink in the dirty water and then turned back to the car.

"Come along to my apartment," he said. "We haven't had lunch yet and I'm hungry!"

Over the meal he passed on certain instructions that I was to carry out, telling me exactly how to deal with Malcolm over the next forty days. He refused to go into the method he had used, and would not tell me why he had found it necessary to break an egg on Malcolm's head. It was such an unlikely thing for Hamid to have done, frowning as he did on all things that had any relationship to magic. Then he gave me another shock.

"Tomorrow I am leaving for Istanbul. By early January you can find me in the southern part of Anatolia. If you come properly, and at the right time, I will receive you. But you must come alone, and leave behind all that is past. If you want to follow the Way, you must leave everything behind. There must be no loose ends, no dirty laundry in the closet, no bills unpaid. There must be nothing to hold you from coming with both hands open. So far, all our work together has just been preparation for this moment. Now it is up to you to take the next step, which is a step completely into the unknown."

He smiled at me then, putting his hand on my arm. "It is true that I know something about the Dervishes. You must forgive me, but the things that we may go into together one day are not for everyone and I had to be absolutely certain that you really wanted to know with your heart and not just with your head. But then I expect you were beginning to pick up on these things already, weren't you?"

He handed me a postcard. "Look carefully at this picture. One day, God willing, you will visit this place; if you do then you will know that your real journey has begun".

The card was a photograph of the interior of what appeared to be a large tomb. In the foreground a magnificent cloth of gold covered what I imagined to be a coffin, at the head of which rested an enormous blue turban. Light illumined the area, reflecting on the colored walls of the tomb, brilliantly covered with gold Arabic script tooled into the red, black, and green tiles. On the back of the card Hamid had written his address, "C/o Post Box 18, Sidé, Anatolia, Turkey."

We spent the rest of the afternoon together. I had not

realized how attached to him I had become, and to our times of study together. The thought of his going away filled me with a sense of loss, but I also knew that to follow him would have profound implications for me for years to come. We embraced before I left him; deeply moved I left the apartment building and walked toward the bus stop. It was a chilly day in November of 1969. The air was damp, with a slight fog. I could smell the burning leaves from a bonfire in the square.

By the time I reached my own apartment I made what was perhaps the most important decision of my life. I had decided that I would somehow or other sell my business, clear up all loose ends, and leave England to join Hamid in Turkey. I went to my desk and wrote to him. Then I wrote to my business partner, who was on an extended vacation in America, telling him that I was now willing to sell my share of the business which he had wanted to buy for some time. I telephoned a real estate office to put my apartment on the market, wrote letters to friends and family, trying to explain my reasons for making the decision to leave England indefinitely, and informed my meditation group what I was going to do. Then, with great difficulty, I wrote to all those who had been coming to me for healing and told them the name of someone else who might be able to help them. The first steps had been taken, and now I had six weeks to get everything prepared properly before I left for Turkey.

Six weeks later I was on the plane bound for Istanbul. I had received only one letter from Hamid, saying that he was looking forward to seeing me, but also enclosing a list of people that I was to visit before meeting him in the south. I was exhilarated and impatient to see him, but apparently my journey was to unfold like a pilgrimage before I could reach my goal.

two

Because I love
There is an invisible way across the sky.
Birds travel by that way, the sun and moon
And all the stars travel that path by night.
—Kathleen Raine

As the flower is the forerunner of the fruit,
so man's childhood is the promise of his life.
—Hazrat Inayat Kahn

I spent my first day in Istanbul just walking the streets, trying to get used to the rush and the noise. Each car seemed to be sounding its horn at the same time, drivers yelling at each other in the traffic jams, and the pedestrians shouting at the drivers. Children pulled at my coat, trying to sell me candy, and on every street corner someone was selling something. There were men with suitcases full of trousers, small boys with shopping bags, and dark-skinned men from Kurdistan who pressed forward with prayer rugs from Lake Van and Anatolia. Women carried cases of plastic kitchen utensils colored shocking pink and green, lucky charms, and baskets of fresh flowers. There were old men who only sold nail clippers, and on corners people huddled over red-hot braziers, roasting corn and fish caught that morning in the Bosphorous. On one side of the street one old man offered his services as a knife sharpener, and on the other there was someone mending typewriters.

At one point in my wanderings I stood outside the Blue Mosque, surely one of the most beautiful buildings in the world, and for the first time heard the call to prayer echoing across the rooftops. It was truly a new world, exciting, exhilarating, and perhaps a little frightening for someone who had never visited Istanbul before. I had walked all day except for the times when, exhausted, I sat down to drink Turkish coffee in tiny cafés where men sat smoking black tobacco in hookah pipes as they watched the bustle of life pass by. Toward evening I was hungry, and in the restaurant situated in the old part of town that I had chosen for my evening meal I decided to order kafta, tiny skewers of meat broiled over open charcoal and served with stuffed vegetables. To my surprise I suffered no ill effects, despite the long years of having been a vegetarian. The change that I knew was to come about must have already commenced!

I slept well that night in the small hotel room I had rented. In the morning, as soon as I had eaten breakfast, I began searching the telephone directory for the name Hamid had given me of a Sheikh—a spiritual teacher—whom I was to visit as soon as I arrived in Istanbul. He had said that I might be able to contact the man through a group called *the Societié Metaphysic de Turkiye,* but that I might find it difficult to pursuade them to give me his address as there was always an air of secrecy about these matters. However, try as hard as I could, I drew a blank. No such society was listed in the directory and I really had no idea where else to start looking. My difficulty was compounded by the fact that I could not speak a word of Turkish. I decided to leave the hotel and head toward Tacsim, the big modern square lined with hotels, travel agencies and airline offices, where at least one person in every office speaks either French or English. I thought that perhaps my instinct would see me through, but wherever I inquired I drew a blank, and by evening I was almost convinced that my task was impossible. If I was not a very stubborn person by nature, and if I had not trusted Hamid as much as I did, I would have given up that night. But something kept me going, and the next day I decided to search in the old part of the city, again approaching anyone who might speak English, asking them if they had ever heard of the Societié Metaphysic de Turkiye.

By noon of the second day I was no further ahead, and although Hamid had instructed me to visit another person in Istanbul as well, he had stressed that it was essential to meet these people in the order that he had given me. I was now on the point of giving up; my feet were sore and blistered and I felt increasingly disillusioned about the whole affair when, on the afternoon of the third day, I went into a barber shop just a few doors away from my hotel to get my beard trimmed. The barber had spent two years working in a Paris hotel, and was delighted with the opportunity to talk with someone who spoke French. We chatted about Paris and London, where he had visited briefly, and then about Istanbul. Just before leaving, I asked him the inevitable question —did he know of the society I was searching for. "Why, yes," he responded casually, "I know the society. If you like I will take you there. . . ."

How could it possibly have been so simple? After searching the city for three days to then find the information I needed in a barber shop only a few yards from my hotel! I tried to explain the circumstances that had brought me here, but the barber merely smiled, pointing out, as had Hamid, that there was no such thing as chance and that surely if it were destined for me to find the Sheikh then I would, and if not, then not. Then he added, "When I was a young man I was involved in these things. But now I have a family and a job that lets me talk to people all day long and I do not have much time to study. They say, however, that the Sheikh who knows the people in the society is a very great man indeed, and I hope that you will meet him. By the way, their office does not open until the evening, so perhaps it would be a good thing if you went back to your hotel and we could meet here again later."

I spent the next two hours in the hotel lobby, reading week-old newspapers that I had already seen in London, waiting impatiently for evening.

The barber arrived at last, and we left the hotel and walked across the square. It was getting dark as we turned down a narrow back street. A cold wind was rising, rain was in the air. People huddled in doorways, their overcoats pulled up round their necks, the light from the street lamps illuminating the steam rising through the gratings over the drains. The barber did not speak to me but hurried along so that I was almost running to keep up with him. I couldn't tell if he had chosen a deliberately confusing route, but I knew that I could never retrace our steps alone.

We reached a small square at the end of a cul-de-sac, and there, on the massive wooden door of one of the buildings, a brass plate identified the "Societié Metaphysic de Turkiye." My companion knocked, and after a short time the door was opened by a woman in her mid-forties. Her dark hair was pulled tightly away from her forehead, knotted in a bun at the back. She wore a simple black skirt and white blouse, and looked not at all the sort of person I had come so far to meet. She glanced at me sharply, then turned to my companion. They spoke together briefly in Turkish. She stepped inside the house and shut the door. The barber gave a little bow and disappeared into the dark street, leaving me to stand alone on the doorstep.

There was just enough time for my apprehension to turn to fear before the door opened again and the woman reappeared with a male companion. The woman, who spoke fair French, began to question me about my reasons for being in Istanbul and about my interest in the Societié. I did my best to answer, but I couldn't be sure what she really wanted to know. Finally she asked, "Why do you want to visit our Sheikh?" I was taken aback, until I realized that my guide, the barber, must have told her of my search. I tried to explain that my teacher had set me this task, but my explanation grew very confused. They did not seem to recognize Hamid's name and continued to question me for several minutes. The woman said abruptly, "We will go now."

We took a taxi and drove through one of the oldest parts of Istanbul. It was late in the evening; the city was a blaze of lights, and the markets still seethed with people. The car stopped in a narrow alley which the buildings overhung so far that it seemed possible for people to lean out of their upper windows and shake hands. We climbed out of the cab, rang the bell of one of the old houses, and waited, looking up at the balcony. After a short while an old man appeared on the balcony, wearing sleeping pajamas. He waved to the group, and indicated that he would come down to let us in. When he opened the door, he was still in his pajamas, but he was also wearing a blue jacket. On the wall at the top of the stairs was painted a beautiful red rose, five or six feet tall. We left our shoes on the landing outside the door, and I walked into the room to meet the first of those to whom I had been sent.

For at least two hours the Sheikh talked to the group in Turkish while his wife sat by the door, occasionally bringing more tea and sweet biscuits. During all that time, he ignored me. He would look at each of the others in turn, but whenever his gaze approached me he would turn his eyes away. As far as I could make out, they were discussing some passage from the Koran. Everyone grew very excited, and every now and again there would be shouts of "Allah." At one point everyone began crying over something that he said. It had been about eight hours now since I had first entered the barber's shop. Perhaps I had made some mistake and would never be allowed to greet this Sheikh and know whether or not I was to be received. He might have read my thoughts, for suddenly he turned to me asking a brief, direct question, which was translated into French for me by the man from the Societié Metaphysic, who was sitting to my right. "Why have you come?" I began to explain, and for a while he listened to the translation as though he were very interested. Suddenly he seemed to grow bored. Lifting his hand, he stopped the conversation. There was a moment of silence and then, looking straight at me, he began to speak. His voice and that of the translator were the only sounds in the room —even the ever-present background of street noises seemed to fade.

"Once there were two butterflies, one in London and one in Istanbul. They flew toward each other because of love and when they met one died. Do you understand?"

There was a pause and he continued. "When the turtle lays her eggs in the sand she scoops out a hole for them, covers them over, and then goes back to the sea. The eggs are hatched through magnetism, not just by the warmth of the sun as people think. For the mother turtle is still linked invisibly to her eggs, even though she returns to the sea. When the eggs hatch, the baby turtles try to make their way to the water. Very few reach their destination. Waiting for them are the birds, which gather to feed on the tiny creatures; and if they do manage to get to the sea, the fish are waiting, for they too know instinctively when the turtles are going to hatch. Of the thousands of turtles that are born very few live to return to lay their eggs."

Looking at me with great kindness, he added, "So you see, the Sheikh does not necessarily know who he is teaching."

The group seemed very happy; some turned to me and shook my hand, others came over and embraced me, kissing me on both cheeks. I was completely bewildered. What relationship did the turtles have to the Sheikh and his teaching? What was all this business about magnetism and the sun? And if I was meant to be one of the butterflies, presumably the one that had flown from London, then was I dead? Or was it the Sheikh?

Before I had time to dwell on these questions the Sheikh

once again raised his hand for silence. He then told the following story.

"Once there was a rose bush. It was carefully planted so that the roots grew deep in the soil that had long been prepared to receive it. These roots were Abraham. As the rose grew it was necessary that it be correctly pruned, otherwise it would eventually go wild and would not fulfill the intention that the gardener had for it. The stem, through the good earth, the deep roots, and the pruning, was straight and strong. That stem was Moses. One day the most perfect red rose that had ever been seen appeared in bud. The bud was Jesus. The bud opened; that bloom was Muhammed."

The Sheikh paused, and turned and spoke to his wife. She left the room and returned with a small glass phial. He pointed to me and she came across the room to stand in front of me. "Take it," he said, "and tell me what it is." I took the phial in my hand and smelled it. "It is rosewater," I replied. "Attar of roses. It is the essence of the rose."

The Sheikh smiled and beckoned me to come and sit in front of him. His presence was overwhelming. He took my hands in his. "Listen to me carefully and on your journey remember what I have to tell you. Now mankind needs the smell of the rose. One day he will not even need that."

Then he bent forward and kissed my hands, raising them together to his forehead. Putting his right hand over my head, he blew out into the room: *"Huuuuu."*

He got up and left the room. The meeting was over. We found our shoes and started down the stairs. Half way down I looked back. The old Sheikh was standing at the top of the stairs, in front of the rose that was painted on the wall. He leaned forward and called down to me. The translator, behind me on the stairs, said quietly, "Look back once and remember. Don't forget the rose."

The man who had acted as translator accompanied me back to the hotel in a taxi. He did not speak and I spent the time trying to puzzle out what the Sheikh's stories had meant. Suddenly my guide turned to me. "Do you understand," he asked, "why our Sheikh used the example of the turtle to explain something to you?"

I told him that I really had not understood much of what had been said, and asked him if he could explain.

He pondered for a moment. "I will tell you a little more," he said finally, "but you must understand that any answer brings about limitation. The truth is on-going and beyond explanation, so it is better to be left with a question than to be given an answer. I can offer some pointers for you, but then it is up to you to think about these things in your own time. First, though, let us go to your hotel and have coffee together."

It was quite late, and the few people still about were walking hurriedly or sheltering from the rain and the cold wind. Inside the hotel it was warm, and we sat in a corner of the lounge near the fireplace to drink our coffee.

"The main point that the Sheikh was trying to make to you—you understand that the story was told especially for you, do you not?—was that you and I, all of mankind, are connected by an invisible thread. So you see, whatever is said or done in one place has an effect everywhere else in the world. But the degree of that effect is dependent on our degree of awareness. You have been looking for a guide to help you on your journey. Actually the guide is always there for everyone, but unless we are awake we never know that it is so. When the Sheikh said that he does not necessarily know who he is teaching, he was explaining to you that every day he sends a message that spreads throughout the world, and if someone is awake enough they hear the call. Even if they never meet our Sheikh, even if they are thousands of miles away, they still may hear the inner meaning of what he is teaching, for energy follows thought. On the other hand, we must remember that the seeds may take a long time to grow. What you are hearing from me now, and what you have heard from our Sheikh, will go on unfolding within you for many years, and perhaps a little more understanding will grow as a result of our meeting.

"The reason that the Sheikh talked about a turtle and not about some other creature is that the turtle is capable of existing both in and out of the sea. She comes out of one world into another to lay her eggs. After they are laid she returns to the world from which she came. Because everything is connected, she is still connected in the invisible world to the eggs that she has laid. This is the magnetism the Sheikh told you of, which along with the power and warmth of the sun finally hatches the eggs. For this to happen it is necessary that there be both the sun and that special sort of energy that comes from the mother to her children. The eggs hatch, but that does not mean that they will all survive. Only those that are strong are able to make their way to the sea, where they may grow large and old and wise enough to be able to return one day and lay their own eggs. Now do you understand a little better?"

"I'm not sure," I said. "I think I'm beginning to see, but it will be a long time before I'll be able to comprehend what all this means. What I still don't understand at all is the meaning of the death of one of the butterflies."

"Ah," said the guide, "that one is difficult if you are not used to our ways, but it is simple if you understand how the Sheikh makes use of stories to illustrate special points. But you must remember that I'm not really 'explaining' anything. You must find your own meaning in what you have heard tonight.

"Of course, you were one of the butterflies in the story, and our Sheikh was the other. He said that the two butterflies flew toward each other, meaning that just as the pupil needs the teacher, the teacher needs the pupil, so that the message may be passed on. The butterfly here is like the soul, but for true understanding to come about there cannot really be two souls. Now perhaps you say 'my soul' or 'his soul,' but for the understanding that you seek to grow within you it is necessary that the idea of your own soul dies so that you may come upon the One Soul. The Sheikh liked you, and when he said

that the two butterflies met and one of them died, he was telling you that there will come a time when all that you think you are will die, and then will come understanding."

He clasped my hand for a moment, and said, "If we meet properly we meet in the heart, and then there is no more you and no more me. Now I must go, my friend. Good luck with your journey. You know it is the only real journey to make in this world."

He stood up, shook my hand once more, and was gone.

It was late when I went up to my room, but I was wide awake, and there seemed to be little point in going to bed. I sat by the window musing over the shadowed silhouettes of the city, the tiled rooftops, the old European buildings, the modern hotels and the dark slender fingers of the minarets that would soon echo with the first call to prayer. I watched until the hawkers began to shout in the dark streets, peddling their wares to those on the way to work. Below me there was a muted jingling and the echo of slow footsteps on the cobblestone street. A man emerged in the half light leading a huge brown bear. He would probably have come all the way from the east of Turkey and now would be taking the animal to dance in the streets or on one of the piers beside the Bosphorous. I pitied the bear lumbering behind him, another performer in this city of contrasts.

As the sun came up I considered how I was to find the second person I had been instructed to meet. Again I had only a name and no address, but Hamid had said that the man worked in a tailor shop in a street of such shops near the main market. Only if I were sensitive enough would I be able to find the right one. I located the market easily, but finding a particular tailor shop seemed impossible. I spent the morning wandering up and down the streets, in and out of shops, watching for some sign to indicate that I was on the right track.

Toward afternoon I found myself in the area of the booksellers. I entered one of the shops at random and was immediately attracted by a scroll, beautifully lettered in Arabic script. The proprietor, hovering at my shoulder, spoke rapidly to a young boy standing beside the counter. The boy ran out of the store, and with many elaborate gestures the proprietor invited me to join him for tea in the back of the shop.

We were seated across the table from one another, sipping tiny cups of sweetened mint tea, when the boy returned with an older man, who said that he would be happy to act as translator for us. The first thing the bookseller wanted to know was why I had chosen that particular piece of script. Did I understand what it said? When I indicated that I did not, the older man began to translate the words for me. It was the opening verse of the Koran, the daily prayer of every Moslem in the world. "In the name of God, the most merciful and the most compassionate . . ." The room was quiet for a moment, and then with smiles and many gestures the bookseller insisted that I take the scroll as a gift.

We had talked for a long time, when the bookseller rose and beckoned me into another room. An old man with a huge domed head stepped forward out of the darkness. "This one is a real Dervish," the interpreter said, and the three of them spoke together in Turkish for a moment. Finally the old man turned to me and raised his hand, blowing over my head, breathing the word *"Hu,"* just as the Sheikh had done the night before.

When we were seated again, over fresh cups of tea, I told the bookseller about my mission, asking if he knew of the Sheikh who worked in a tailor's shop, but he merely shook his head. "But how am I going to find him?" I asked plaintively. "I've walked and walked and I can't even find the street with the tailor shops and I don't speak any Turkish." He smiled at the desperation in my voice and stood up, signalling that the meeting had come to an end. The interpreter also smiled as he translated the words of the bookseller. "There is a saying of the prophet Muhammed (peace and blessings be upon him): 'Trust in Allah, but tether your camel first.' Perhaps you have not worked hard enough on yourself, for if you had then Allah would most surely guide you to him." I thanked the two men, and as I walked away the proprietor called out to me, *"Salaam aleikhum"*—peace be with you.

All that day I tramped around the market area, asking in English and in French and attempting to use my Turkish phrase book, looking for the street of the tailors. The scene took on a dreamlike quality; I felt detached and distant, as though this search might not really be happening at all. Toward the end of the afternoon, as the sun went down behind the Blue Mosque, and the last call to prayer echoed out from every minaret in the city, I decided to give up. If it had been the right time, perhaps I would have found the man. I knew that I had made my best effort that day, and I felt that if it were really important for me to meet him I would be given another chance.

I was exhausted by the time I got back to the hotel, with barely enough energy to wash and meditate briefly before collapsing on the bed. The bus left the terminal for Ankara, my next stop, at 6 A.M.

three

The tale of love must be heard from love itself.
For like a mirror it is both mute and expressive.
—Mevlana Jelalu'ddin Rumi

Delight is the secret. And the secret is this: to grow quiet and listen; to stop thinking, stop moving, almost to stop breathing; to create an inner stillness in which, like mice in a deserted house, capacities and awarenesses too wayward and too fugitive for everyday use may delicately emerge.
—Alan McGlashan
The Savage and Beautiful Country

Turkish buses may be the only buses in the world in which the conductor walks down the aisle with bottles of cologne to pour into the hands of the passengers. I settled myself toward the back of the bus, enjoying the smell of cologne, ignoring the heated discussions and gossip of the other passengers; all I wanted was to get to Ankara, where I was to pay my respects to a very great man—a saint, in fact, according to Hamid. In England, a few months before, Hamid had instructed me to study very carefully a sentence this man had spoken: "There is no creation in the relative world; there is only the becoming of Being."

"In that sentence," Hamid had said, "is contained one of the great secrets. One day, *Insh'allah*, God willing, you will come into Being; you will be the drop that becomes the ocean. Then, and only then, will it be possible for you to 'do' anything. Until you understand the omnipotence of God, you will always think that you are the cause of something. Do not think that you can choose. Do you really believe that you chose to become my pupil? Something called that we might be together. Know what it is, who it is, that called, and you may come upon the beginning of the Way."

When the bus pulled in at Ankara I checked my luggage at the station and hailed a taxi to take me to the address I had been given. There was no time to waste; I wanted to spend as long as I could at this man's house—assuming, of course, that he would let me in. Hamid had continually emphasized that I must be aware and respectful—and not to be disappointed if I were not received. "Some teachers are for some pupils of the Way and some are for others, and so there is no blame if you go on your way without meeting some of those you were sent to visit. The key is to go with the right intention—they will know the degree of your sincerity."

We drove through the back streets of the old part of town, arriving finally at a square on top of a hill. The area was crowded with parked cars, and lined with shops selling religious books and strings of prayer beads. People were hurrying into the mosque, the men putting on their skull caps and performing the ritual ablutions in the fountain by the gate. The call to prayer must already have sounded.

The driver pulled up by a garden at the side of the mosque, took my money, and before I could ask him to show me the house of the man I had come to visit he was gone, speeding on across the square and back the way he had come. I stood for a moment in the winter sun, looking out across the city, and tried to get my bearings. The last of the faithful had entered the mosque and the leather curtain had been let down.

I walked across the square to the shops. In the first one the owner was praying on a mat at the entrance. The second also was kneeling in his doorway, but the proprietor of the third greeted me in English. "You are American." It was not a question at all, but rather a statement. There seemed little point in saying that I was English. "My friend has a son who studies in California, in Berkeley. He is studying physics but my friend is very unhappy because his son writes in a letter that he is going to marry an American girl who is not Moslem. And he also says that she does not even know that you must wash before you pray."

He continued his monologue. "The trouble with Westerners is that they do not understand the meaning of the ritual ablutions. It doesn't matter if they are Christians or Moslems, if they are believers in God, then how can they learn to pray without knowing how to wash?"

"Tell me," I interrupted. "Do you know Haji Bayram Wali?" He looked at me in much the same way as the taxi driver had done, and became solemn. "There is Haji Bayram Wali, may God bless his secret," he said, pointing to the mosque. "He made his pilgrimage to Mecca many times. One day I too hope to go there."

With that he embraced me. "How wonderful it is that an American from Berkeley, California, should have heard of the great saint." I explained that I had been told to pay my respects to him on my way south to visit my teacher, and that I had been given a special sentence to contemplate before coming. When I repeated the sentence to him he became even more excited, and ran out of the shop to summon his friends as they emerged from the mosque. A dozen or more men crowded about, shouting *"Musselman, Musselman"*; then they almost carried me out of the shop and across the square toward the mosque. So I was to meet their Sheikh! My sense of exhilaration and anticipation matched the enthusiasm of my companions.

At the edge of the mosque was a gate, and beside the gate was a fountain where they all stopped to wash their hands, feet, and faces, encouraging me to do the same. Then the man from the shop spoke with someone standing beside a low door, and we entered the room. When my eyes had adjusted to the light I saw that the walls were covered with finely written Arabic script.

"Haji Bayram Wali," announced my friend. It took a little time for me to realize that I was inside a tomb. Those words of Haji Bayram Wali had been so real and present for me that it had never occurred to me that he might have died centuries before.

Somehow it was clear to me what I must do. It is said in Islam, "When you pray, pray with your hands." I opened my hands, palms raised like the others standing beside me. I had no idea what prayer of this sort might mean, but I felt that if only I could open myself totally I might begin to understand. As I did I felt a tension in my throat, and at the same time a tremendous burning in the center of my chest. I started to weep, and as the tears rolled down my face I knew, in a language beyond words, what it means to be received by someone who had reached into a world beyond time and space. It was no more a question of his being alive or dead. In this sort of prayer you are transported into a different dimension altogether. I stayed a long while in the mosque.

When I came out into the sunlight I realized that I had been allowed to take another step, and that on this extraordinary journey Hamid had marked the map well.

That same evening I was on a bus again, bound for Antalya, the last stop before joining Hamid at the address he had given me in Sidé. I had sent him a telegram informing him that I would be there soon, and as I got closer and closer to my destination my excitement increased.

The bus pulled into Antalya shortly after noon. Across the street from the bus station I saw the office of a travel agent, and decided to inquire about the next bus to Sidé. I carried my bags across the steet and made my request known to the owner of the agency, who spoke French. Nothing in Turkey happens quickly; we spent several minutes chatting, then I told him that I was going to be in Sidé for some time, visiting a friend. "He is English?" I was asked. "No," I said, "Turkish, from Istanbul, but he spends a lot of time in London." "Ah," said the man, and then lapsed into silence. After quite a pause he said, "You are English?" "Yes," I replied. "Ah," again. Another pause. "To get to Sidé you must take a car or a Jeep, that is, unless you want to wait for the bus tomorrow." "Then I will stay here for the night; can you give me a hotel room?" "Ah, but you see, when the sun goes down, it *is* tomorrow, and tomorrow is the last Wednesday of the moon. So it would be better if you went now, this evening, before the sun goes. It is not a good thing to make beginnings on the wrong day. But then, you probably don't believe in these things." It was a question.

The last Wednesday of the moon! Hamid had explained to me that Islamic countries use the lunar calendar, rather than the Western solar calendar, and that certain days, most particularly the last Wednesday and the thirteenth day of the moon cycle, are traditionally considered most unfavorable for the commencement of a new undertaking. If I were to arrive properly, I definitely must make my way to Sidé today or else wait until Thursday.

The man behind the counter interrupted my train of thought. "Is your friend very tall, and big, and does he have glasses, and a mustache?" "Yes, yes," I stammered, "do you know him?" "No," he replied, "but ten minutes before you arrived a large Turkish man with a mustache and glasses came in and asked if I had seen an Englishman with a red beard." Smiling at my excitement, he instructed his assistant to look after my luggage and took me out into the street. "He went that way." He pointed down toward the sea. "Go quickly—perhaps you can find him."

I ran down the street, peering into shops and glancing up alleyways. I came to the seafront and stood in the cold wind. There were only a few old men strolling along, and the street dogs skulking close to the buildings, searching for food. Perhaps I was too late; already it was the middle of the afternoon. I felt near panic as I ran up another street. Still nothing.

Once or twice I thought I saw him, but always he was just going round the next corner, and when I got there he would be gone.

Finally, heart pounding and chest aching, I retraced my steps to the travel office. The owner came out to greet me. "Ah," he said once again, "just as you went down the street that way," he pointed to where I had been, "your friend walked in from that way." And he pointed in the other direction. "Now he is in the coffee shop across the street, having tea. We will go there." And picking up my bags we walked back to the place where I had first arrived in Antalya.

I did not see Hamid when we entered the cafe, but then he was walking quickly toward me. We embraced so warmly that I cried with the relief of meeting him again.

"Good," he said, "you are just in time. Welcome to Turkey. There is a car waiting—we will leave at once. We must reach Sidé before the sun goes down."

The man from the travel agency waved good-by to us when we drove past his office on the road to Sidé.

As we drove through the olive and tangerine groves the afternoon sun dazzled the blue expanse of the Aegean. Whole families were returning from the fields—the men on donkeys, the women and children walking alongside. Some of the donkeys were so laden with baskets or mounds of hay that only their legs were visible beneath the huge loads. Everywhere dogs ran and played, snapping at each other's legs. Some of the women were veiled in full purdah, the skirts of their long black dresses blowing behind them in the breeze. It was a scene that had not changed in fifteen hundred years. It was natural, at peace with the moving harmony of the land itself.

We reached the edge of the village shortly before sundown. "There is quite an impressive view from the cliff over there where we can pay our respects to the beauty of the sunset," Hamid said, pointing out the window of the car. "Just by the cliff, hidden behind the hill, is an ancient Greek amphitheater. Soon perhaps we will explore it. But now you are tired, and tomorrow is the last Wednesday of the moon."

We climbed up the side of the rock, the wind blowing in from the sea bringing a chill into the air. At the top of the cliff face I realized that we were actually standing on the remains of one of the great walls of the amphitheater. Looking down, I could see directly into the arena. It was as though time had reversed itself, for everything was just as it had been left by some long-forgotten earthquake. Great pillars were piled like fallen trees, haphazardly crushed against one another. There had been no excavation that I could see, and I felt as though we were the first human beings to witness the scene since its abandonment. The ground where we sat was strewn with fragments of marble caps and broken sections of pillars. Huge lava formations jutted up from the beach, red and orange in the dying sun. Outlined against the sea, Hamid sat with his knees raised and hands folded. He seemed to be deep in thought; his lips were moving slightly and his face reflected an intensity that I had never seen before.

Suddenly Hamid stirred. "I must take you home before dark." We walked silently along the beach back to the car, a chill wind at our backs. "You have had such a long trip, you must be very tired. Tomorrow you will rest; and tomorrow night, when Wednesday is over, we will meet again and have a wonderful dinner in the town."

It was a short drive to the house which had been lent to Hamid by a friend of his who lived in Istanbul. The two-floor house was built so that the rooms faced out over a courtyard on three sides. On the fourth there was a high wall which afforded complete privacy. In the center of the courtyard was a beautiful tree whose branches hung down to the ground, similar to a willow. It was lit by lamps hanging in the branches, and around it were beds of flowers. The portion of the house opposite the door through which we entered the courtyard was more modern than the rest of the house and Japanese in style, being long and low and made of pine. There were two identical rooms, one on top of the other, with a short flight of wooden steps outside leading directly to the upstairs room. Downstairs the curtains were drawn, and I saw the flicker of a match as a candle was lit, and the shadow of a figure move across the window.

"That will be your room—the one upstairs." Hamid pointed. "Come and we will take your bags up together."

The room was perfect. It was simple and clean, with a tiny shower built into a corner. There was a chest of drawers with a pitcher of water on it, a lamp beside the bed and another on a table by the window. The table also held a bowl of flowers and a copy of the Koran in English. "Don't keep the light on and the door open," he warned. "The mosquitoes here are quite voracious. I am used to them, but you are fair, and they are particularly fond of European skin. Good night." With that he left me, walking back across the patio to his quarters above the kitchen in the other house.

I lay down on the bed and immediately fell asleep. I must have been more tired than I knew; I slept for twelve hours. The next morning I washed and then breakfasted on the bread, cheese, and fruit that Hamid had set out for me. I spent that day quietly, sitting in my room or wandering in the garden. It was a dreamlike day. I was content, almost like a child, to drift from place to place, to look at a house, a fence, a heap of stones. I was not really aware of the passage of time. Once I glimpsed Hamid at the window of his room above the kitchen, but he did not seem to see me. After sundown he appeared, smiling. "Take a shower," he said. "There is water tonight. Then we will dine together."

We walked a short distance down the street to the little restaurant in the square. It was the only one in Sidé. Obviously the village had been warned that a foreigner was coming to stay, for a table had been set overlooking the Mediterranean, and a special menu had been prepared. The owner of the restaurant came to sit at our table, and soon we were joined by several of Hamid's friends. I suppose I had thought that on my first night in Sidé Hamid and I would talk about my experiences on the journey, but after the first introductions he and his friends spoke to one another in Turkish. I might as well not have been there at all.

Food was brought, dish after dish, and carafes of rough Turkish wine. Once or twice I heard my name mentioned and hoped that I was about to be included. The conversation continued, however, while I looked out at the glistening water, ate what was given to me, and wondered what would happen next. Perhaps I had come on the wrong day after all. I knew better than to interrupt, of course; I was sure that when the time was right, the conversation would come round to the things I wanted to discuss. In the meantime, though, I was growing impatient. My mind went back over the previous day, my arrival in Sidé, my new room, and the one below it—the candle I had seen being lit in the window . . .

I became aware of a growing sense of dejection and loneli-

ness, so intense that I was afraid that I would break down right there at the table. I struggled to regain my self-control, but I could not rid myself of a feeling of great pain which grew stronger as I saw a figure walking across the square toward us. At first I could not make out the features, and then I saw it was a beautiful woman, tall and dark. Her black hair hung below her shoulders. She wore a long white dress, her feet were bare, and in her hands she held a tangled mass of blue wool which was twisted around her wrists so tightly that her hands and arms, which she held out in front of her, were bound together. The owner of the restaurant got up quickly and fetched her a chair. Hamid led her to the table, gently unravelled the wool from about her wrists, and poured her a glass of wine. She was beautiful—so delicate and ethereal that she seemed hardly of this world. I realized that the sense of loneliness I felt was emanating from her.

The woman bowed her head very slightly as Hamid introduced us. She did not speak, but again picked up the blue wool and started to fumble with it. Her hands moved slowly and carefully at first, her fingers searching through the tangled mass. Then they became agitated, frantically plunging into the blue of the wool.

Hamid spoke to me, though his eyes never left the young woman. "She is looking for the end," he said. I held out my hand to try to help her, but he touched my arm, signaling that I was to leave her alone. Presently he bid good night to the others at the table, motioned for me to follow, and led the woman across the starlit square. We walked silently together along the shore back to the house. Just before we reached the house she turned and stood for a moment, looking out to sea. I could just make out a loop of wool trailing down beside her. Then she turned and went through the door. Hamid and I watched her cross the courtyard and then the light of a candle appeared in the window of the room below mine, glowing through the mosquito netting, faintly lighting the tree by the stairs.

Hamid turned to me. "Come to my room tomorrow morning at seven o'clock," he said. Then he embraced me, kissing my hands and putting them to his forehead, and walked toward his room.

four

I died from minerality and became vegetable;
And from vegetativeness I died and became animal.
I died from animality and became man.
Then why fear disappearance through death?
Next time I shall die
Bringing forth wings and feathers like angels;
After that, soaring higher than angels—
What you cannot imagine,
I shall be that.

—Mevlana Jelalu'ddin Rumi

All is contained in the divine breath, like the day in the morning dawn.

—Muhyi-d-din Ibn 'Arabi

Dawn broke over the hills, waking the dogs in the village, opening the day. I heard the call to prayer from the minarets —*"Allah Hu Akbar, Allah Hu Akbar":* "God is great, God is great." The call of the muezzin echoed over the rooftops five times each day, summoning the people to turn, once again, to God.

I performed the ablutions, as Hamid had taught me in London. He had said, "If you do not have water, then wash with sand; and if you do not have sand then wash with a stone; if a stone is not available, then cleanse yourself with intention so that you approach the moment as free of the past as possible." I washed very carefully that morning, praying that I would be open to receive whatever might be given.

Promptly at seven I knocked at Hamid's door. He was waiting for me in the room. He gestured for me to sit on a chair facing him, and without preliminaries he began to speak. "This morning I am going to teach you a little about breathing. I am sure you realize that breath is the secret of life, for without breath there is nothing. With correct breathing it is possible to choose the way you wish to travel. Think of the wind—it blows and carries with it whatever is light enough to be lifted from the earth. It carries the scent of flowers, it carries the leaves as they fall from the trees, and it carries the seeds from the plants to the place where they may take root. There is a great message here! We come into this world on the breath and we go out of this world on the breath. The average man, living his life in a mechanical way, forgets all about breathing until the moment of his death when he struggles to draw air into his lungs, clutching to the last remnants of what he has known as life in this world.

"The practice I will give you this morning can be done every day, every moment, for the rest of your life. It seems easy, but as each moment is different, each day is different, and at times you may find it impossible to concentrate. But little by little you will come to understand the importance of what I am telling you.

"First, you must learn how to purify the subtle bodies by surrendering the concept of the physical body so that you may come upon that invisible matrix from which the body is continuously being formed. If you learn how to purify yourself, you will be able to see more clearly for the thought forms and projections that obstruct clear sight and inner hearing begin to dissolve. After all, thought is the only thing that divides us."

He instructed me to move my chair as close to his as I could. Then he took my hands in his, with my right palm up and my left palm down, forming a circuit through which I could feel a spiral of energy moving between us. The effect was immediately calming.

"First make sure that your back is straight, and then simply watch the rise and fall of the breath. To be able to do this takes much practice, and few people are prepared to make the necessary effort. When you can just watch the breath you will begin to realize that we are tyrannized by thoughts that move us this way and that almost constantly; and although we do not like to face the truth, it becomes clear to us that we have little of permanence. But you are *not* your thoughts, any more than you are your emotions or your body. If you are not your thoughts, and yet you find it so difficult to just watch the breath and not be moved by these thoughts, then is there not something wrong?"

He put more pressure on my hands as he asked this question until I looked up into his eyes. "Listen carefully," he said, "and remember this—until you have a permanent 'I' you will always be in danger of being led astray. When you learn to breathe in awareness, then there is a chance to come upon this inner being that is your real self.

"Today I am going to introduce you to three aspects of breath. The science of breathing is the study of a lifetime, but these three aspects—if considered carefully and put into practice—can help change the course of your life. They are the rhythm of the breath, the quality of the breath, and the positioning of the breath.

"Much has been written recently in the West about the rhythm of breath, called *pranayama* in India, but people do not realize that the different kinds of rhythms taught by different schools and teachers are meant to produce different results. If you want to drive a car very fast up a hill, the engine takes on quite a different rhythm than when it is coasting gently down the hill. The speed of the car may be the same, but the rhythm of the engine is quite different. It is the same with the science of breath—the understanding of rhythm is vital.

He paused, and I was not quite sure whether or not he wanted me to respond. Before I had time to reply he went on. "The rhythm I am going to teach you today is sometimes called the mother's breath. People do not realize that something is being 'born' out of every moment, and that if we could find the rhythm that is most natural and most in harmony with the universal laws governing our existence, we would be contributing to the work of bringing about peace on this planet.

"So this is the first lesson, to consciously practice a very basic rhythm of breath. Make sure your spine is straight, so that the vital fluids can pass easily up and down. Now, inhale to a count of seven, pause for one, and breath out for a count of seven. Before breathing in to start the second cycle, pause once more on the out breath for a count of one. This is a very simple rhythmic count of 7–1–7–1–7. If you work hard the timing will soon become automatic. Now practice this rhythm with me."

As I relaxed and surrendered to the rhythm I began to feel very light. Hamid was still holding my hands, and I could see the rise and fall of his abdomen as he breathed. Although the rhythm was strange, and rather difficult to follow in the beginning, something in me started slowly to awake—an observer who was able to watch all that was going on and yet was not identified with the rhythm itself.

"Good," said Hamid. "Now trust a little more, relax and close your eyes, and just allow yourself to be breathed. Let go of all concepts—surrender to the rhythm that flows and pulsates throughout all life. This rhythm is called the law of seven, and by following it you establish yourself as part of the harmonious principle of life which wishes only to conceive perfection from within itself.

"Now as we come to the next stage, which is concerned with the quality of the air you breathe, you are to continue with the 7–1–7 pattern.

"Just as the wind carries on its wings whatever is light enough to be lifted from the earth, there are many qualities that can be carried on the breath if we understand rhythm, and if we are able to concentrate correctly. For example, you could choose one color out of the whole spectrum and breathe it into your body, infusing each cell. This practice is useful in certain types of healing. You can breathe in a strong vibration, similar to the low notes of the piano, or you can choose to breathe in the finest vibration imaginable which, in this world, would be beyond the range of sound. You can choose anything! You could breathe in the elements of fire, earth, air or water. You could breathe in the essence of a particular flower or herb in the same way that you breathe in the perfumes of flowers and know the difference between them. The science of breath is a vast subject, known only to a few in the past, but now it is time for the world to begin to understand. With the correct rhythm, and with the knowledge of what I am telling you, extraordinary things can be done!

"But these are only hints along the way. When you have practiced sufficiently the basic rhythm, we will be able to talk in greater detail.

"The third aspect I wish to touch on today is the placing of breath. Just as the wind carries the seed from one place to another, so the breath can carry intention from one area of the body to another for special purposes. Through correct placing of the breath we can learn to bring the body into balance. We can begin to learn the art of transmutation, the art of the alchemists. We can begin to fulfill our responsibility in being conscious human beings devoted to a life of service on earth.

"Now breathe with me, feel the rhythm I have taught you, and be infused with the finest quality of air that you can imagine. Be purified with this air. Let it wash away all your pain in this moment. As I breathe with you, feel the energy spread down from the top of your head, and pass right down through your body."

As I relaxed, and allowed my body to breathe as Hamid directed, I felt an ease, a new sense of freedom that I had not experienced before. At the same time I had to struggle not to lose concentration and awareness. Hamid held my hands tighter.

"Now I want you to take several very deep breaths. Each

time you breathe in, consciously attune yourself to be in balance, and at the same time take responsibility for your body. You have managed to let go of a lot of what you thought you were in order to discover something real within yourself. This is what we call the observer. You must learn to develop this observer a little more each day. You are here to learn to be in charge of the vehicle that you have been given. Stand proud in this world, but bow in the next."

I breathed slowly and deeply, and soon Hamid instructed me to open my eyes. The room looked quite different, as though I were seeing it for the first time. I felt a tremendous sense of peace and security. All was in its proper order. I sensed a perfect flow between the objects in the room, and through each object itself. There was a sense of communion, of acknowledgement—the chairs, the table, the bed, all knew of each other. They were not inanimate objects any more, but part of living Being. Everything had awareness, spoke a silent language. Everything was, in Essence, perfect.

Hamid took his hands away from mine and stood up quietly. He walked around behind me, held his hands above my head, and slowly brought them down on either side of my body, two or three inches away from my clothes. Then he stood beside me and made the same actions in front and behind. Finally, standing behind me once more, he put his hands on my shoulders and told me to be quite still. A tremendous heat poured through his hands, so that my whole body tingled. He stayed there only a few seconds, and then sat down once more. "Good," he said, "now when we begin to talk about the real world, it will be easier for you to understand. But first we must have coffee and breakfast. Can you make Turkish coffee yet? You can't?" He shook his head sadly. "Well, you must learn, and then each morning it will be your job to fix it after the meditation we will do together. When we have had coffee and breakfast, we will sit and talk. Now you should go down to the beach for a walk, and when you come back I will have prepared the coffee for you."

With that he left the room. My body felt strangely weak

and it was hard at first for me to move from the chair. I rested a few minutes more and then set off down the path to the sea, to watch the fishing boats returning with the morning's catch.

As I walked along the beach I thought of the change in Hamid. This morning had not been like the times we had spent together in London. I felt a sense of authority in him, a no-nonsense attitude that left no room for compromise. Before there had always been time to talk about mundane affairs, to laugh a little, and to share in a dinner table discussion, but now there seemed to be a sense of urgency. I felt that I was expected to extend myself beyond anything I had ever attempted. Certainly I had taken this leap into the unknown, but now I realized there was no turning back. I had put myself into this man's hands. The play had begun, and I didn't even know the outline of the plot.

When I returned from the beach, Hamid had set the table for our breakfast on the patio. The meal was held in silence and after we had cleared away the breakfast things, Hamid gestured me to precede him into the house. When we were again settled in our respective chairs, he began to speak as though we had never left.

"During the time you are here we will have a period of study every morning. This will be new for you, as Westerners seem to think that study is a way of assimilating information, or of gaining knowledge. But you cannot gain knowledge. Remember that—knowledge cannot be acquired, it must be given. It is given to you at the right moment, but really it is all there within you. Education comes from the Latin word *educare,* which means to bring forth. It does not mean to stuff down some extraneous bits of information from some outside source. The study I mean is the study of essential truths in love and in awareness so that what is within you, waiting to be born, may begin to unfold. If you study hard, understanding will grow out of itself. But before you study in this way you must always prepare yourself; that is why we do the practices first. You have to learn to balance the three worlds —the world of thinking, the world of feeling, and the physical world. Study is not a—what do you call it?—a head trip. If you study just with the head, then you end up with concepts of the truth. If you study just with the world of feeling, then you could walk around in a state of perpetual halleluyah, feeling everything but with no direction. If you just do physical exercises to train the body, then you may get so earth-bound that you will never aspire high enough. It is a question of balance.

I interrupted him to ask, "What do you mean when you say that knowledge is given and not acquired?"

"Be careful. That is a mind question. It is not a true question. If you were listening to me properly, you would not even think of asking such a thing. You still think that you are capable of *doing* something. You have really learned nothing yet. I have told you to listen, to let what I am saying sink in, not to start trying to explain with the discursive mind. You will study by listening. If you do not wish to listen, then go away—and come back again when you are ready. I have plenty to do and I do not care to waste my time. Waste is the only sin and everything follows from that. Sin is a lack of knowledge, so if you want to understand you must listen."

Taken aback by the sternness of Hamid's response, I realized that I had asked the first question that had popped into my mind, simply to get him to stop talking for a moment, to give my rational mind a chance to catch up with what he was saying. I had not really considered my question at all.

"Please forgive me," I said. "I didn't mean to interrupt. I only wanted to understand. Please go on—I'll do my best to listen."

"I'm sorry I spoke so sharply," he said. "This is only your second day here in Sidé, and you are weary from traveling. But you must remember that it is different here than in London. There we worked around each other, having a good look at one another, both of us deciding whether we were going to take this next step together. Then you were offered the chance to come, and you accepted the offer. Now you have come to my house, and each moment counts. I want you to stay here for the least possible time; we have no time to waste. I want to pass on to you some of the knowledge that I have been given, so that you can go back and teach others." He paused. "Devotion to God is studying Him in every aspect, understanding God is knowing all you can of Him, serving God is teaching what you know of Him to others. For now, you trust and learn, and study. And study, and more study."

"Are there any books you wish me to read?" I asked.

"Certainly not," he replied. "You have read for years, and where has it got you? You head is filled with masses of ideas and concepts, and you yearn for experience that others on the path have had. Before your true nature is understood all those ideas and concepts must melt away. No books—the only book is the manuscript of nature, the lesson is life itself. Live passionately! Who said that this path should be so serious that there is no joy in it? This is the most exciting adventure possible, and it should be enjoyed. Joy is the springing forth of knowledge, *knowing* that God is perfect and is beyond comparison. Do you remember that I once asked you why you were vegetarian, and I told you that I ate meat because I know that God is perfect?" He smiled at me, and there was a twinkle in his eye that made me smile too.

"I knew what sorts of thoughts and questions you would have, but I never asked you to change to my way of thinking. Always we ate together the sort of food that you felt was right for you to take. But now the time is coming when it will be necessary for you to realize that, as there is One Absolute Being from which all stems, so we cannot separate anything from that One Being. Everything in this universe is perfect and of proper order. It is part of the play of life, that animals are given to us for food, so that we can live. It is part of the redemptive process. It is only through mankind that redemption can take place. The process is alchemical, and we are merely transformers of subtle energies. A very great teacher, Mevlana Jelalu'ddin Rumi, said, 'I died as a mineral to become a plant, I died as a plant to become an animal, I died as an animal to become a man. I will die as a man and rise in angelic form. Why then should I fear to die?' Who is the 'I' here? Is it not the great I, the first I? Contemplate on these things today.

"Within you is everything that has ever been, and everything that will ever be, all past time, all the different kingdoms. Do you think that the animal world is any different? Look at the animal. It eats the grass, and the grass has already taken into itself the minerals of the earth, the sunlight, and the other energies of the cosmos. So, by eating the grass, the animal has absorbed both the mineral kingdom and the vegetable kingdom into itself. There is only One Absolute Being. This means that we must accept responsibility for the way we breathe. Remember this, and know that whether you eat meat or not, every time you inhale you are breathing in the elements that are contained within the animal world. Even as you breathe now you are inhaling some of the air that I have already exhaled; when you were vegetarian you were breathing in the elements of the meat I had eaten, transformed through me. Were you aware of that?

"As I told you this morning, the secret of life is breath. Through correct use of breathing there is nothing that cannot be transformed, and it is our duty and our obligation in being born to become conscious transformers.

"I'll tell you a story about how this can work. A young woman once came to me who had traveled a great deal in India. For one whole year all she had eaten was oranges. That's true—oranges and nothing else. This woman was immensely strong; she could carry a heavy pack on her back. Logically she should have been completely wasted away, but she was actually healthier than most. She came to see me because she had heard that I might be able to introduce her to certain people in the Middle East. I had invited her for lunch, not knowing her eating habits. Although she was very polite, she was horrified at what we were eating. There were fourteen of us around the table, and I had cooked duck, basted in the oven with curaçao and Grand Marnier. Someone had brought a fine claret, and we finished the meal with champagne and a lemon souffle. She excused herself, said that she was on a special diet, and brought out an orange from her bag which she ate very slowly. Most admirable it was, but in her horror at our eating habits she was not able to hear what was being said. During the course of the conversation, I gave two names and addresses to the group, knowing that was what she had come for. She did not hear, for she was caught in a concept of how a spiritual guide should be, what he should eat, and so on. She left very disappointed, and more than that, angry with us.

"The inner secret of the story is this: she had had a teacher in India with whom she had studied for a long time. He was an ascetic and taught her the diet that she followed, but more important than the diet was the breathing which she studied with him. Through the correct use of breath she was able to take in all that she needed. She did not know it, but she was taking in everything that was necessary from the different kingdoms—'I died as a mineral to become a plant . . .' Do you understand?"

He waited in silence. I opened my mouth to ask him another question, but this time I was frightened.

"I can see that the question you are going to ask is from the heart, and so I will do my best to answer it."

"What I wanted to ask, then, is if it's possible to take in all that you need from eating an orange and correct breathing, why do you still eat meat?"

This question seemed to strike him as uproariously funny, for he leaned back on the sofa and laughed, his body shaking, and he went on laughing until the tears poured down his face.

"Oh, you Westerners," he said, "why can't you understand? I eat meat because I like to eat meat."

The meeting was over. He left the room without a word, disappearing into another, smaller room that was separated from where we had been sitting by a rug hung across the door frame. I waited for a while, and then walked across the patio to my room. I had decided to spend the afternoon on the beach. I was to meet Hamid at sunset by the Greek amphitheater, so I had plenty of time to rest, and try to assimilate what I had been told.

So much had happened since my arrival two nights before that I had almost forgotten the beautiful woman who had joined us at dinner. She came out of her room. She held her hands in front of her, just as she had the night before, the blue wool again tangled and knotted about them. I felt embarrassed by my intrusion into her world and at the same time I felt overwhelmingly sad. She walked toward me, not looking directly at me, her head slightly tilted and her hands and fingers pointing toward my chest. She was so intent on her action that I backed away in sudden fear. I felt that she was trying to possess me and yet I could not look away from the hands thrust toward me. The palms were joined as in prayer, and the blue wool hung in tangles to her waist.

When she was within two or three feet of me, she raised her head and looked into my eyes. Trying not to take my gaze from hers I reached down and carefully pulled away the wool from her hands. As I untied the last strands she smiled, looking at her hands in front of her as though for the first time. The mass of wool trailed down onto the ground. I bent to pick it up. As I did so she screamed, and went on screaming, crying out in pain. She fell to her knees, clutching the wool in her hands again.

As I reached out to help her Hamid appeared, hurrying across the courtyard. He pushed me aside and bent down, putting his hands over hers. Immediately the screaming stopped, and as she looked up at him she was like a very young girl. He took her hands and helped her up, motioning to me that I was to collect the wool. As I rose to hand it back to her, he took the wool, bent and kissed it, and gave it to her.

Then he put his arm around her and led her to the house.

I followed them slowly across the courtyard and went up to my room. Who was the young woman? I had never heard her speak—perhaps she couldn't. The compassion with which Hamid treated her, the extraordinary gentleness he showed when he led her to the house, made me think that perhaps she was his daughter. But it had not been the right time to ask, and I was learning that it was better not to inquire about things that did not concern me directly.

So much had happened since I had arrived in Sidé that I was sure I had not absorbed a fraction of what I had been given. I tried to remember if Hamid had ever said anything during our talks in England about the subjects we had discussed that morning. A sentence that I had heard him say at a dinner party in London flashed into my mind: "Man is a transformer of subtle energies. The 'Work' that is our work on earth is the art of translating the point with no dimension into dimension for the reciprocal maintenance of the planet. . . ."

I couldn't remember the context of the sentence that had stuck in my mind, but I had left his apartment that night wondering what the "point with no dimension" was, and who or what constituted the "Work."

Toward sunset I walked along the beach to the place where I was to meet Hamid to watch the sun go down. Everything was deserted; except for three fishermen mending their nets by the café, I was alone. I had not seen Hamid since before lunch, and no sound had come from the room below me. The girl must still be with Hamid.

I waited a long time by the rocks, but no one came. It was quite dark before I finally decided to return to the house to see what had happened. Lights were burning in the windows, and I heard dishes rattling in the kitchen. I knocked and went in. He gave no explanation of why he had not come, and I didn't ask. He indicated that I was to sit down, and placed a bowl of black olives, some white cheese, and a glass of wine in front of me. "Eat," he said. "Dinner will be a little time yet." I watched him cutting vegetables by the stove, noting the intensity of each movement that he made. It had been the same in London. He never spoke when he was preparing food, for he said that it was such a sacred act that it was necessary to do everything in awareness and respect. "Be grateful for all that gives you life," he would say, "and make yourself good food for God."

I ate some of the olives. They were quite extraordinary, unlike any olives I had ever tasted, and I wondered where he had obtained them. When he had finished preparing the food, I asked him about them. "Ah," he said, "to get olives like these requires a very special process." He sat down with me, and I poured him some wine. "Let us toast the olives," he said, "for these olives went through a lot to become as delicious as they are." Then he began to laugh, great belly laughs that shook the table. "You had the same olives many times in London," he said, "why did you not notice them then? But if you had, then maybe you wouldn't have had to come all the way to Anatolia to find out about them.

"To prepare olives like these the first thing you must do is to buy the very best quality you can find. Then rinse them carefully several times so that all the salt is washed away. You understand?" I nodded, making mental notes so that I could fix some in the same way. "Next take a jar that you have washed carefully—it must be perfectly clean. Into it put the washed olives, and over the olives pour boiling water. The olives will swell. Leave the water on them just long enough for them to expand—but not too long, or the skins will burst. Then pour away the water and add some slices of lemon and some fresh mint. Finally you fill up the jar with first pressing olive oil, the purest you can find, which is the essence of olives. Screw the lid on the jar very tightly and leave it for forty days and forty nights. Then they are perfect. Mind you, they are pretty good after seven days."

He was roaring with laughter again, as he watched me trying to memorize the process. "Come on," he said, "set the table and let's eat. The olives can wait until tomorrow."

We talked far into the night. He would not discuss the events of the day, and to all of my questions he would say only, "That is another matter," or, "The time is not yet right to discuss these things." He told me wonderful stories about the Dervishes of Turkey and Persia. "You may meet some," he said, "but there is no need for you to go and find them. If your intention is clear, someone will come to you. Keep awake, though, or you will miss the moment."

Before I left him for the night, he said that we should pray. I tried to explain to him that I did not understand prayer, that I could not see the meaning or purpose of it. "Then pray that you will understand," he said impatiently. "Devotion is necessary in our path. The trouble with you is that you don't believe in God. You only think you do. If you knew what I know, then you would pray, but the prayer I am talking about is beyond form. And where is your love and your gratitude? How many times a day do you remember to say thank you? You are completely dependent on God and it is to Him that all thanks are due. Until you can be truly grateful you will always be in separation from God. You have forgotten about prayer because you have forgotten your dependence on Him, so that prayer has become a mere vain repetition of words. That is not prayer. The prayer of which I speak is the prayer of the heart, the state where all life has become a prayer. You should get up in the morning in praise of Him, and you should go to sleep in grateful thanks for all that you have been given. He may come with a thorn on which you tread to wake you up. He may come as the gentle wind, or the rain. However He comes, and whatever He brings, it is necessary that you are grateful and that you acknowledge Him, for praise and gratitude are like the two hands of prayer."

He was silent for a long moment. "A great Sufi once said, 'Make God a reality and He will make you the truth.' Begin now, this evening, to understand the meaning of this. Do you not want to meet God face to face?"

Feeling rebuffed and ashamed, I began, very quietly at first, to acknowledge my thanks. It was as though the words had been waiting for release. They took on their own rhythm.

There was response. From the gratitude came a joy that washed away the tensions and the questioning. The response was so immediate that for a moment I doubted and opened my eyes. Hamid was still there, sitting opposite me. As I closed my eyes I felt the release again in my heart.

We sat in silence for some time. When finally I rose to go to my room, Hamid smiled at me as though from a great distance. We did not speak again that night.

five

Behind every "O Lord" of thine, are a thousand "Here am I's."

—Mevlana Jelalu'ddin Rumi

Soul receives from soul that knowledge, therefore not by book nor from tongue.
If knowledge of mysteries come after emptiness of mind, that is illumination of heart.

——Mevlana Jelalu'ddin Rumi

The next morning, as usual, I went to Hamid's room at 7 o'clock, but he was fast asleep. In fact he was snoring, a deep rumble from beneath the bedclothes. The room was littered with books and papers, and I guessed that he had been up most of the night. Just by his bed a pile of papers, more neatly stacked than the rest, caught my attention. The heading on the first sheet was, "The Way of Service and Surrender—A Treatise on the 13th Century Sufi Mystics." Under the heading was a quote.

The earth and the sand are burning. Put your face on the burning sand and on the earth of the road, since all those who are wounded by love must have the imprint on their face, and the scar must be seen. Let the scar of the heart be seen, for by their scars are known the men who are in the way of love.

—Prophet Muhammed
(Peace and blessings be upon him)

Not for the first time, I wondered about Hamid. Apart from the evenings I had spent with him in his London apartment, his life was a secret. Sometimes I tried to probe for information, but he would always lead the conversation away, indicating that his life was his life and that it was not for me to ask questions. His insistance on privacy was so great that I really had no idea who he was.

Was Hamid a Dervish, I wondered. The papers stacked beside his bed intrigued me, and I bent down to have a look. The rumbling snore still emerged from beneath the covers, and although I knew that I was invading his privacy, the temptation was too great to be denied.

I was just about to pick up the top sheet of paper when Hamid woke up. For a moment he did not notice that I was there. Then, seeing me bending over the papers, he sat bolt upright in bed, his face contorted in anger. "What are you doing here? Have you learned nothing? You come into my room without permission, and you have the gall to look through my things! What else have you done? What else have you been looking at? Go on, tell me."

I assured him that I had been in his room for only seconds, and that I had not touched anything else. I stammered that I had not wanted to wake him, but since he had told me to be there at the usual time I hadn't known what to do, whether to go or to stay. I felt physically ill with fright and shame.

"Enough!" he interrupted my explanation. "You have made a bad mistake, and ordinarily I would throw you out of my house. In our tradition it is necessary to be scrupulously honest, and to respect the dignity of the human being more than anything else. You are young, untrained, and British, and for that you have been allowed to make several mistakes, but now you must learn. From now on you will not enter my room without first obtaining permission, and you will not ask questions unless you are invited. If you are careful, and if you act properly, then we can continue together. If not, I will find someone else. You are not important, you know. You may be a useful vehicle, but you can be replaced very easily. Is that understood? Now go and make coffee and breakfast and leave me alone until I call you."

"I'm sorry, Hamid." I said. "Please, please, forgive me."

"Out!" he shouted. "No time for sentimental nonsense here. We have work to do, and if you wish to learn, then you must get on with it and not carry on about old mistakes. It was right that you said you are sorry but do not expect pity."

As I made the coffee I realized that I had indeed sought pity instead of being able simply to apologize and to know that the moment had already passed.

About half an hour later I heard Hamid shout from his room. "Come," he ordered, "and bring the coffee with you."

His hair was still wet from the shower, and he welcomed me as though nothing had happened. "Well," he asked, "what have you learned?"

The question was so unexpected that I had no ready reply. He had done this often before, and each time I fell into the trap. He would allow me to have some concept of what was going to happen next, and just when I felt at ease with the situation he would come up with a statement or an action that destroyed any continuity of understanding. Once, in London, I had asked him about this. He had replied, "To come upon the Way it is necessary to break the clock. You must destroy your pattern of comparisons."

I was silent for some minutes, trying to come up with an answer that would please him.

"I don't know how to answer you," I began. "I've only just arrived and so far I've been so disoriented that I don't know *what* I've learned. It's all so new—perhaps it will take a few days before things have sunk in enough for me to be able to answer the question."

"Nonsense," he said. "You are just stubborn and lazy. If you would only listen and trust, you would be able to answer me.

Surely you must have learned something." He accented the last word and bent forward, looking at me hard between the eyes.

"Well?"

"I've learned that I really know nothing, and that only now am I at the beginning of the journey. Before this moment everything has been just preparation."

"Everything is always preparation," he said, "so that is no answer. We are preparing now for the world to come, but when it will come is in the hands of God, not in our hands. We must always be in a state of preparation. Preparation is the art of staying awake. If you are awake then one day you may see into the real world. You cannot expect to come into that world if you walk around like a sleepwalker in a dream. Nearly all the world is asleep, but they do not know it. You cannot wake up by reading books that tell you you are asleep. You may not even wake up just because a teacher tells you that you are asleep. You can only wake up if you want to, and so begin to work on yourself to cut away all the rubbish in order to come upon the nature of who and what you are. Waking up is not a question of some supernormal experience, either. I have met many people who call themselves psychics who are even more asleep than those who know nothing at all about these things. These deluded people think that if they can contact some sort of 'guide' they are excused from doing any work on themselves. They merely cover up their own pain with yet another set of illusions.

"The only thing to be done is to come to know the Unity of God; then everything is given. If you try to find pieces of Him, aspects of the One Reality, then you are caught in the pieces, and where is the Unity? If you stop on the journey to admire the flowers you may forget the object of the search, and instead remain with the flowers. Certainly they are beautiful, but what do you want? Always observe your own motives most carefully—look closely at what you are doing and why you are doing it. Search incessantly for your true nature, but not *for* yourself. Do you understand?"

I was listening, and felt that I did understand at least some of what he said. If you try to develop the self (whose existence you do not truly know) then you are developing an illusion. Only when you work on yourself for something greater than the mind understands can it be said that you are doing anything useful or constructive at all.

I explained my feelings to Hamid. He seemed pleased, and said, "Ah," several times. Finally he interrupted me to ask, "Did you really enjoy the olives?"

Once more I was taken off guard. "Why yes," I said, confused. "I told you last night how good I thought they were and asked you to tell me how to make them so I could fix some myself."

"But you didn't truly enjoy them if you didn't understand them. Did you understand them?"

What could he mean, understand them? They were wonderful olives, certainly, but how can you understand an olive? I searched desperately for an answer while Hamid sat watching me impassively, sipping his coffee. At last, looking exasperated, he said, "You are not so completely stupid as to think I was talking just about the olives, are you? Do you really imagine, after all this time, and after all the things I have said to you, that I would waste my time just talking about olives? Sometimes I despair of you. Listen, for God's sake. You are here to learn, so go and clean out your ears and stay awake. Any story that I can tell you can be understood on many levels. If you were just on the level to hear how to make good olives, that is one thing; but you should be able to go beyond that, and anyway I would not have told the story unless I knew that you could understand. Now listen carefully.

"The salt that preserved the olives in their sacks is the conditioning of your life. It must be washed away before any true work can be done. In order to obtain the best results, you must choose the best olives, of the finest quality. The olives may be seen as the many aspects of yourself; or, each olive could be said to be one person who is potentially useful to the Work. They say that 'many are called but few are chosen.' The jar, which must be carefully cleaned in all ways, is either your body or the space occupied by you or the group. Water takes on the color of the vessel that contains it, and we want this water to be as clear as a mountain stream. That is why ritual washing is so important. But we have already talked about this.

"The olives are very delicate after the cleaning away of the preservatives so they are placed into a jar carefully and with loving kindness and, of course, awareness. Next comes the boiling water. That is the first baptism, the baptism with water. It is a total immersion which is, in one sense, in the relative world, very painful. You must understand that this path requires conscious suffering. Remember that the rose bush can produce a perfect rose only through correct pruning. The pruning may hurt the plant temporarily, but if the plant were able to understand the necessity, then it would be filled with joy each time the gardener came with the knife. If we enter this path, then we must recognize the necessity of the suffering.

"The water is left in the jar only long enough for the olives to swell. The skin must not break, for if one olive spoils, the others will be ruined. The cook must know how long the water should remain in the jar, and at what temperature.

"Now the cook adds lemon and mint. Such a good blend of flavors! You should try it with roast lamb—delicious! It is a perfect blend of acid and alkaline, positive and negative, yin and yang. With the final addition of olive oil, the olives come into balance. This last part of the operation is the second baptism. It is the baptism of the Spirit, the essence of the olives themselves. This is alchemy, you see, and it is a great riddle. You must add something to the melting pot, the cauldron, that is the very essence of what you are cooking. Then you screw the lid on tight and leave it for forty days and forty nights, the length of time necessary for certain aspects of the creative process to take place. At the end of that time everything should be in balance and blended nicely together. The lemon and the mint will have blended with the olive oil, and the flavors of the flesh of the olives and the oil, mixed with the other ingredients, will have become as one. The cycle is complete, and everything is returned to its source."

Then he smiled at me, acknowledging my amazement. "You see, it is necessary to look beyond the apparency of things. There are indeed some real cooks in the world and, if you could eat the food that they have prepared, you would receive all that is necessary for the growth of the unawakened man into the man who sees with the eyes of the universe and hears with the ears of the winds and touches with the hands of God."

There was silence for a moment. The surf was breaking on the rocks and I could hear a dog barking in the square. In that silence there was peace—and yearning. I wanted, more than ever before, to die to everything that had been within my own insulated and self-involved mind, to come into something pure, into knowledge. I wanted to be able to return to everyday life with something to say of the real world, something that would be of help to people.

Hamid was watching me carefully. I could find nothing to say, but he seemed satisfied. "Good," he said, "now you are coming upon a little knowledge. However, it is true that a little knowledge is a dangerous thing, for it leaves you so vulnerable that you may easily be knocked off the path. On the way to discovering your true nature it is possible for you to be opened, or to open yourself, to an invisible world, far more powerful than the world you can see with the normal senses. You may think that the atom bomb is a powerful thing, but that is nothing to the power of the elements. These matters can be spoken of only when you are much stronger, however, and when you are in a state of true conviction. Anyway, your body is too weak just now because you doubt so much and are so obstinate. The body always loses energy and becomes weak when there is doubt. When there is true belief, all the energy that we need is available to us. You have a long way to go yet. Starting tomorrow you are to work more on your body. Because you were a vegetarian for so long, you must be careful of your protein intake. When you are involved in the Work, you need more protein than usual, for you need to be able to burn anything that comes into your magnetic field.

"When you are with me and we are open, and working together, that is fine; but when this is not so, then you must eat well, sleep well, and make love well." He looked at me out of the corner of his eye, and I felt that he was telling me something that I could not hear.

"When you come to sit with me, prepare yourself and be open to what will be given to you. At other times go out and enjoy the sunlight and fresh air. Do not dwell on these subjects, beyond following certain instructions that I may give you.

"I will tell you another story. In London there lives a very fine teacher. She owns a restaurant and is there most days, but few people know who she is and what she knows. Once I heard her tell a young man, who was also a student of mine, 'Oh, you listen to me, friend. Traffic in London plenty bad. Too many cars on the road, people angry and not polite to each other. Cars go and crash, and all sorts of hurt come. You got to learn to drive your car now that you have just a little, little knowledge. Me—I'm a very good driver. I drive my car. I do not bump into other people's cars even if they bump into each other. I drive my car and I watch, and so I make the right move. Remember the traffic very bad now, all over the world. You must learn to be a good driver when you are on the road.'

"Do you think she was just talking about automobiles?" Hamid asked. "No, she was talking about the traffic in the invisible world, which is on the increase. It is increasing because it is angry at not being recognized. And so human beings, not knowing the nature of things, find themselves moved this way and that, and before they can get back in control there is a crash, and it is a miracle if they are not hurt. Listen to what I say, and pray that you may understand, and then remember what you have understood."

With that he stood up, stretched, and to my surprise, belched loudly. I realized that the lesson was over.

"Now it is time for lunch, and it is also time for you to relax. We will drink some raki, and then perhaps have a nap on the beach. Have you ever drunk raki?"

"No," I answered. "I don't even know what it is."

"Then you have a surprise waiting for you." His eyes twinkled and he did a little dance on the carpet, turning round and round with his arms outstretched, his hands and fingers moving and swaying like an Indian temple dancer's.

"Only the men dance down here," he said. "Perhaps you and I will dance together. But then you are so British and you might get the wrong idea!" He roared with laughter, and then, still chuckling, embraced me. "Don't worry," he said, "you have a lot to learn, and dancing would do you good. I shall try to get hold of the Gypsies from the next village. Ah—the music they play! We will have freshly broiled fish, and you will meet my friend Mustafa. He is in love, and when he is in love he sings like an angel. Indeed. We will have a party and as the planets turn so we will turn. And you, my friend, will learn to be a man and to behave like a man."

"There is one thing that I must ask you." I hesitated before going on with the question. "Please, who is the girl in the room below me?"

He turned around sharply and faced me. "I told you," he shouted, "you are not to ask questions unless the time is right, unless you are given permission. When the time is right you will be given what you need to know. This is my last warning. You are *not* to ask about things that do not concern you. And what's more, you're a fool!"

I followed him down to the café in the square. He walked quickly, looking neither to the right nor left, and I did not know whether I was expected to go with him or not. I hurried along six or seven paces behind him. When we got to the café the owner came running out to greet him but Hamid brushed him aside. He sat at a table overlooking the fishing boats and shouted for a bottle of raki to be brought. I waited just at the edge of the area where the open-air tables were set out, until he ordered another glass and motioned me to sit down in front of him. He poured the colorless liquid into the bottom of each glass, and filled the glasses to the brim with water. The liquor turned a milky color, like absinthe. Without further words he raised his glass, touched mine, and drank the contents in one draught, signifying that I was to do the same. I took a deep gulp. It was horrible! It burned my throat, sent shivers up and down the back of my neck, and made my tongue curl up. I tried to smile at him but my jaw was locked into position as though I had just come from the dentist. Hamid had already filled my glass again. "Drink it," he commanded. "In one gulp this time."

What sort of spiritual teaching was this? With one shuddering gulp I drank the contents of the glass.

When I was able to breathe again, I looked across the table at him. He had already poured himself a second glass and was talking to the waiter in Turkish. Without turning around to look at me he poured some more into my glass, filled it up with water, and went on talking. I sipped gingerly, loathing the taste of it, and yet not wanting to offend Hamid, who seemed to be vastly enjoying himself. The liquor had a strange effect on me. The visible world seemed to become flattened into two dimensions until, finally, I realized that I must be quite drunk.

"What's wrong with you?" he demanded abruptly. "Can you not drink—and you an Englishman? There is nothing wrong with alcohol taken in moderation. But you have drunk too much on an empty stomach. That is foolish."

"But you gave me the drink!"

"And what has that got to do with it? Have you not been given the choice to take it or not as you wish? You had the choice, but you went ahead and drank something that you were not used to, and now you are quite drunk. Isn't that very silly? You must learn to be discriminating and, if necessary, to disobey. Now go and choose the food you want from the kitchen. I have already ordered mine."

I was suddenly very angry. This was plain manipulation. He had put me in a position from which I could not escape, and then he accused me of being stupid. What was he playing at? In London he had said that it was not a good thing to drink more than some wine at dinner, and here he was downing great gulps of this filthy tasting liquor, and telling me that I should not do so. Yet he had told me to do it. . . .

The alcohol had made me dizzy and had also released a lot of anger that I had not been aware of previously. In the kitchen, where I went to choose what I wanted from the great steaming pots on the fire, I found myself shouting at the waiter who was hovering about with a notebook, explaining to him in English that I didn't know what I wanted, I didn't much care, and I wished I were back in London where things were done quite differently.

Not knowing what I was saying he smiled at me patiently, and when I finally pointed to some of the dishes he wrote everything down and led me back to the table.

"And, well?" Hamid started again. "What have you learned from all this? Perhaps if you have another drink you will be able to see a little more clearly."

He poured another glass and passed it over to me. I drank it down without complaint this time. I could hardly taste anything anyway and I was on the verge of letting go completely and shouting at him, the waiter, the restaurant. Everything was starting to turn round and round, and suddenly I felt it was time to dance.

"Let us dance," I said to Hamid, staggering to my feet. "I have the urgent desire to dance. Perhaps you will teach me the Turkish way."

I moved to the center of the square. Hamid did not move a muscle. He just sat there eating his lunch.

"Come on," I shouted, "let's all dance." I almost fell into the waiter's arms as he came up to me. Swinging him about in an old-fashioned waltz I spun him across the floor toward the table. I tried with my free arm to catch hold of Hamid.

"Everyone must dance together. How wonderful it is to be alive!"

Then, with one final burst, I stumbled into the table and collapsed at Hamid's feet with the waiter spread-eagled beside me.

The shock sobered me slightly. The waiter, laughing, brushed off his clothes, but there was an ominous silence from Hamid.

He stood up, towering over me as I lay on the ground trying to get the world into focus.

"That," he said, "was the most disgusting performance I have ever seen. Did I not tell you that you should not drink? Go home to bed at once."

Somehow I made it home and collapsed on my bed. The raki created a strange state, half dream and half hallucination, in which I was overwhelmed with fear and guilt. I couldn't be sure whether I had really behaved so badly at the restaurant or whether the whole scene was just a fantasy; either way, the sense of loss and dejection made me question once again my purpose in being here.

Unbelievably this was only my third day in Sidé; I had lost all sense of time. A day with Hamid was not measurable in hours. Time was constantly being shattered. Shocks broke the cycle of normal living. I was never allowed to become complacent, to argue with myself, or to justify my own confusion. One confusion followed another in such quick succession that my mind, accustomed to linear thinking, soon reached a state of bewilderment. "Divine guidance," I suddenly recalled Hamid telling me, "is to bring a man to the point of perplexity."

But still with the bewilderment came overwhelming fear that my mind would split. Could I face what lay beyond mind and consciousness? The only hope, it seemed, was to trust so absolutely that the fear which obscured the reality of experience would melt away. Perhaps, if I could be free of this, I might be able to hear and see clearly enough to understand what lay behind this extraordinary journey. But how to be free? Hamid had told me that, paradoxically, on the path of knowledge those who doubt the most become often the best gnostics. To trust and to doubt at the same time—to abandon oneself to the unknown and at the same time to question each moment so that the motive is always clear—how could this be possible?

Lying on my bed in this raki-induced half-waking state, I realized that what I was experiencing was the fear of the unknown rather than the familiar fear of rejection. Everyone who enters upon the spiritual path does so because of a rejection of some sort; otherwise there would be no search. If one feels totally accepted, what is there to look for? The fear of the unknown, on the other hand, is something that everyone must come to grips with sooner or later. I realized that I was locked in that fear. Perhaps that was why Hamid had gotten me drunk—to loosen me up so that I could face the problem. Immediately I began to feel better—until I realized that I was making excuses again, finding yet another subtle way of refusing to surrender to something greater than myself. I decided to go for a walk on the beach to clear away the hangover and then go and see Hamid as soon as possible.

The beach was empty, and a chill wind swept in from the ocean. I ran the length of the beach and climbed to the top of the amphitheater. Looking down into the ruined arena, it was easy to imagine the days when the Greeks and Romans lived in Asia Minor, when the games that were played in this very amphitheater involved the use of human beings as bait for starving animals. How much change had there been in two thousand years? The same questions were still unanswered. Perhaps there were no answers.

A movement behind me and to my left interrupted my thoughts. I felt suddenly embarrassed, as though I were an intruder, and pretended to be examining one of the broken pillars. *"Merhaba,"* said a voice. "Greetings." I turned to see an old man sitting just behind me on one of the seats. He was smiling, and held a basket of eggs partly covered by a cloth.

"Merhaba," I replied, eliciting a quick flow of Turkish. I smiled apologetically and tried to explain in half-remembered phrase-book Turkish that I couldn't understand him. He looked very serious and said "Ah," several times. Then, looking at me searchingly, he inquired, *"Musselman?"* Remembering my instructions, I bowed my head slightly, put my right hand on my heart, and said, *"Alhumdulillah"* —"All glory to God."

With that he moved down to sit beside me, shaking my hand fervently. Although quite taken aback, I tried not to look too embarassed, and as he was talking continuously I could only look at him and nod in agreement. "Allah," he announced. "Mahommedah Rassoul-allah." Then, putting his hand on his heart, he stated, "Dervish, Dervish."

I stared at the old man, realizing that I had finally discovered—or rather, been discovered by—a real Dervish! "Dervish," he repeated for a third time, and continued to speak rapidly in Turkish. The only familiar sound in that flow of words was "Mevlana." Each time he said it he would pause and look at me inquiringly. I would nodded and smile eagerly, even though the content of his words was beyond my grasp. Then he took my hand in his and kissed it. Moving close to me on the stone seat, he took my right hand in his left and began to chant, his body swaying backward and forward from the waist, his head moving rhythmically from side to side. *"Hu-Allah,"* he chanted. Strangely, his voice was at once thin and resonant, as though the sound came through him from a great distance. He stopped and looked at me expectantly. "Hu," he said, putting his right hand on my heart. "Allah." He raised his hand to my right shoulder. Somewhat shakily, I began to chant with him.

"Hu-Allah, Hu-Allah." As my body responded to the rhythm, each syllable seemed to take on an existence of its own, as though the sound and I were one, a channel for the outpouring of some greater force. I felt the Hu high in my throat, like a fragment of the ocean captured in a sea shell;

Allah reverberated in my heart, deep and forceful. I heard and felt the sounds, but they came forth effortlessly, as though I had tapped into a dimension that had always existed and allowed it to flow through me for an instant.

The joy that I had first felt at this unexpected meeting gave way to a deep inner love, and to a conviction that indeed there is something beyond the mind; there is God; there is truly a source of all life. My fear was gone, leaving in its place a complete trust in the moment and in this old man beside me.

He changed the chant to the single word Allah, calling out the name of God with such fervor that he nearly pulled me off the rock seat. The air inside my body was compressed down into the solar plexus and then up into the heart, exploding from my heart into the world on the second syllable of the word. The phenomenal world, my body, the amphitheater and the beach—even my own past had vanished, swallowed up in the Name. There was no future, there was just this moment.

Thc sweat was pouring down my body and both of us were shaking. I was carried into worlds of light and sound that erased all pain, all doubt and suffering and fear. Suddenly I felt his hand squeeze mine and realized that he had stopped chanting, and it was only my own voice that I heard. I tried to open my eyes but I could not. I heard him give a long call, gentle as the wind. He let go of my hand and rubbed the back of my neck. When I opened my eyes he was sitting just in front of me. There was so much love pouring through him that I could hardly look at him. Saying "Hu" once again, he bent down and touched his forehead to the ground, signaling that I was to do the same. Then he took both my hands in his, kissed them, and raised them to his forehead in the same way the Sheikh had done in Istanbul. For a while we sat in silence and then he got to his feet and bent to help me up. "No, no," I protested, but he took my arm firmly, dusted off my clothes, and led me down the steps to the beach. There he bowed deeply from the waist; with a word of farewell he turned and walked off down the beach. I turned in the opposite direction, to go and find Hamid.

The sun was setting when I got back to the house. The questions I had planned to ask Hamid that evening had gone from my head. Instead, as I entered the house, I found myself incapable of saying anything at all. Hamid looked at me searchingly and gave me coffee. "You have been sleeping?" he asked. I shook my head and tried to speak of what had gone on that afternoon, but the words wouldn't come and all I could do was to smile apologetically and sip my coffee. There was no hurry, and we sat in silence for a long time. Finally I was able to explain what had transpired.

Hamid listened intently, occasionally questioning me about specific details of the afternoon. When I had finished, he asked, "Well, do you know what all this means?"

"A little," I answered. "I know that Allah means God, and that Hu means Him. I have heard that Hu is the first manifested sound in the universe. But when I used to ask you about these things in London you wouldn't tell me anything at all."

"The time was not right then, but now that you have been granted such a gift we will talk of these things for a while. Tonight you may ask any questions you wish."

Instead of waiting for my questions, though, Hamid continued to speak. "The first and most important thing you must learn is the meaning of the word *zikr.* It is an Arabic word that literally means 'remembrance,' and it is a daily practice for all followers of the Way. There are many ways of performing zikr, and the one that you were given today, the sound of Hu-Allah, is used by many of the Dervish orders. From what you told me of the old man you met this afternoon I learned that he is a Mevlevi Dervish, a follower of Mevlana Jelalu'ddin Rumi, whose seat is in Konya. This means that soon you must go to Konya to pay your respects to Mevlana."

Without giving me a chance to ask about this proposed trip

to Konya, he continued. "You may wonder why it is necessary to perform zikr, particularly since you are not an orthodox Moslem. The answer cannot be given easily. First it is necessary to know the meaning of zikr on many levels, and then you will find the answer for yourself. The full zikr that all Moslems say is contained in the words, *'La illaha illa 'lla'*, which means, 'There is no God but God,' but the Dervish says, *'La illaha 'illa' Hu,'* which means, 'There is no God but Him that is God.' This tells us that when we have negated our own separate existence, and affirmed the everliving presence of God, there is still a further reality, beyond the beyond.

"We are not involved with religion, or with form. We are involved with the inner meaning, the inner stream of truth that underlies all religion. Our way is not a way for those who cannot go beyond form. It is for those who wish to go straight to Essence. In zikr the orthodox say, 'Allah-Hu,' 'God-Him;' but the Dervish says 'Hu-Allah.'

"There are many ways of performing zikr, and the teacher must seek the level of the pupil so that he will give him the correct type of zikr. You must not take away form if the pupil still needs form. The rule is, if the pupil is not ready to go beyond form, then give him an exercise." He laughed, leaning far back in his chair.

"But it is necessary that you learn about zikr," he went on, "for it is only possible to know the truth if you are in a state of continuous remembrance, if you are always awake. I can only teach from my own experience, so I will instruct you in remembrance of God through zikr. Other traditions, of course, have other methods of remembering, like the continuous repetition in the Christian way of the Jesus Prayer—'Lord Jesus Christ have Mercy on me.' But you must never compare ways, or feel that one is better than another, for that judgment only causes separation and disharmony. What is important is the attitude of remembrance. If it comes only from the head, then nothing will happen. Only when zikr is repeated in the heart will your prayers be answered.

"You may wonder why I am instructing you, a Westerner, to do zikr in Arabic. The answer has to do with sound. Arabic is the closest living language to ancient Aramaic, the root of both Hebrew and Arabic, and the sounds themselves have certain properties that are not translatable into any other language.

"For the present, you are to continue with the special form of zikr you have learned today. Every day you should contemplate on the meaning of the words. The full meaning of the words 'La illaha illa 'lla' Hu' is 'No, there is no God but Him that is God.' You begin with denial, denying everything so that only He remains. This means that you give up your little will in favor of the greater will, the Will of God. When you have done this, you affirm His name with the cry of 'Allah' and then, if you are very still, and empty of yourself, you may hear His reply—'Hu.' 'I am, that I am.' It is the reply of the beyond of the beyond, the sound of the overflowing of the Divine Essence, beyond all attributes.

"Tomorrow morning you will begin. First you are to contemplate the meaning of the words, then repeat the full zikr, La illaha illa 'lla' Hu, thirty-three times, and follow it with the zikr of Hu-Allah, as the old man taught you, for as long as you can without losing concentration in the heart."

After promising that I would begin the practice of zikr in the morning, I asked Hamid if he knew the old man and where he had come from. "Does it matter?" he demanded. "Why are you always so inquisitive? The fact is that he was there and you were there—both in the same place at the same time—and so you met. I don't see that it matters who he was. The moment is gone now. And who knows—perhaps the old man wasn't there at all, but only in your imagination."

"But I saw him, and he taught me the zikr," I protested.

"Ah, but is not everything inside you?"

There was a long pause. "All right," he said finally, "that was a little hard. But one day you will understand that what you experience within manifests itself in the outer world, or the mirror, so that you can see yourself in the mirror. No, I don't know who he was. Perhaps he was just passing through. They do that sometimes. Or maybe he was taking the basket of eggs to his family. If it is right, you will meet him again, but if it is not right, then you will not meet him. You must always remember that there is only One Absolute Being, and so whether you meet this Dervish or whether you meet another, in reality you are just coming upon another manifestation of the same Being. Do you understand this yet? You see, no two moments are ever the same—that is the miracle of life. Oneness is not a miracle, it is the diversity of the One that is the miracle. What a wonder it is to know that as God never manifests himself in the same way twice, so each moment is an act of total creation. Do you remember I once said to you that time is the eternal attribute of God?"

Once again I experienced a sense of shock and of time distortion, as though Hamid's question had jolted my mind beyond its present-moment capacity.

"What I don't understand, Hamid, is how and why all these things are happening to me. It's all so strange, and there seems to be no logical explanation for it all. Things keep happening—like the Dervish appearing on the beach—and yet you act as though nothing had happened."

"But nothing *has* happened," he interrupted. "How could anything happen? What do you mean by 'happen' anyway?"

"I mean that all these events are taking place, one after the other or maybe at the same time, and I don't know what is going on, or who or what I'm looking for, or even who or what is looking."

"Excellent," Hamid looked quite pleased. "When you reach that point where you know nothing and know that you know nothing, you can begin on the path. All I can do is to help set up the situations for you to come to that point. In reality, of course, I do nothing, for there is only God. We are His players on the stage that He set so that He might see Himself. You should take as a daily contemplation the sentence from the *Hadith* of the Prophet (peace and blessings be upon him), 'I was a hidden treasure and I loved to be known, so I created the world that I might be known.' "

I tried to follow what he was saying, but the harder I tried the more tired I became, and I realized that my mind just could not follow what he was telling me. I asked if there were any more coffee.

"But perhaps you would like some raki now that the sun has gone down?" He laughed and went to fetch the bottle. "I would rather not," I said, "I don't want a repeat performance of this morning."

"But you must learn to control yourself. If you don't have a drink now, how will you know if you can? As I said to you before, there is nothing wrong with alcohol in moderation. Have a drink." He poured me a glass. There seemed to be no point in holding back. "Just one then," I said, and we drank in silence for a moment, while I worked up the courage to again ask the question that was always at the back of my mind.

"Since you said that I might ask questions tonight, may I ask you once more—who is the girl in the room downstairs from mine?"

"I said that you could ask questions," he replied, "but I did not say that I would answer them. It is not the right time to talk about her, but I will tell you that she has been very ill and I am looking after her. On the way to self-knowledge there are many dangerous pitfalls as illusion is stripped away to reveal the essential nature of our being. A teacher who does not know what he is doing, or who has developed certain powers without the necessary experience or knowledge, may cause the veils to be stripped away before the time is right. Then there is nothing left for the pupil to hold onto. The girl is just such a case; but there is more to it than that. She is waiting to be recognized. Do you understand at all what I am talking about?"

"Do you mean she wants to be recognized as a woman?"

"I mean that she is waiting to be recognized as all women. The ball of wool is the blue of the matrix of her world. She is searching for the thread that will lead her back to where it all began. I wonder how many people there are in the world who are in the same place." He gave me a sidelong glance, and I realized that I must study this question on many levels. He never said or did anything without a purpose. I was silent, trying to work out the answer he wanted from me.

"Don't you yet realize that all women are in the same position? Until the woman is recognized by man she can never be completely free. Man has forgotten too much. Yet if he recognized the woman he would free himself. He would become complete. The woman, the earth, has been waiting so patiently, but it may be that her patience is running out.

"This girl has been sent to us so that we may try to help her, but also as a warning and as an example. Be kind and careful with her. She is fragile, but there is a chance that she may one day find the end of the ball of wool.

"This evening I want to be alone, so please amuse yourself as you choose. Tomorrow we leave on a journey."

"But I thought there was to be a party tonight."

"There was to have been, but that was then. Now please leave me. If you see the girl, and if she has not eaten, then take her with you to the restaurant. I will see you in the morning."

I did not see her that evening. I hoped that she would appear in the courtyard, but the blinds were drawn in her room, and when it grew dark no light came on. She must have gone out somewhere. I ate alone in the restaurant, thinking about the day and making notes of some of the things that Hamid had said. Sleep came easily that night.

six

Trust in Allah—but tether your camel first.
—Proverb

If thou wilt be observant and vigilant, thou wilt see at every moment the response to thy action. Be observant if thou wouldst have a pure heart, for something is born to thee in consequence of every action.
—Mevlana Jelalu'ddin Rumi

The next morning Hamid was waiting for me with the usual Turkish coffee, fruit, and bread laid out on the table. After eating in silence he announced, "Today we are going to drive across the mountains to the northwest. I wish to visit the ruins of a temple dedicated to Apollo, and you might as well come along with me. We must start fairly soon, as it is quite a long drive, and either come back late this evening or stay the night somewhere and return in the morning. We will see how the time goes. It will be a day of relaxation and enjoyment after the intensity of the last two days. Go now and get ready."

As I walked back across the patio the blinds of the downstairs room parted and I saw the face of the young woman. She smiled, and then opened the door. Her hair hung down to her waist, and she wore a pale blue nightdress. "Good morning," I greeted her.

She did not seem to hear what I was saying, for there was no reaction in her face. I had forgotten to ask Hamid whether she was able to speak, and so I asked her if she had heard what I had said. This time she nodded her head, and again a shy smile appeared at the corners of her mouth.

"We're going away for the day," I said. "Do you need any help? Is there anything I can do for you before we go?" She stood in the doorway, touching the handle, staring at me. After a few moments I became very uncomfortable. "Well, then I'll see you tomorrow," I said, and hurried up to my room to throw a few things into my overnight bag.

It was nearly noon before we set off in the car. Everything had taken much longer than I had expected. Hamid had disappeared into the little side room behind the curtain for a couple of hours. I had piled the old Mercedes with provisions for the journey, enough for several meals if necessary, as we would be traveling across some very wild country.

The car was very old, and although the engine worked well enough the brakes were bad and the tires were quite bald. As we started out I expressed my doubts about the length of the trip and the condition of the car. Hamid was irritated. "Trust, trust," he said. "Put your trust in God and don't worry. We have done all that we can with the car, and so what more is expected of us?"

In one of the small towns we stopped in an outdoor café for coffee. Sitting beside us was a young man in his early twenties; inevitably he struck up a conversation with Hamid. Although they spoke Turkish, I gathered that the conversation had to do with our trip. The man explained something with many gestures, sketching an invisible map on the tablecloth with his fork. Eventually he shook hands with us both, excused himself with many bows, and left the café. "What was that all about?" I asked. "He tells us that a new road has been opened just this past week and that it would save us at least two hours of driving. Apparently it goes over the mountain, while the old road goes down the valley. He said that it is a very good road, a little steep at the top, but the car would certainly make it with ease. If we don't take it, then we will have to stay the night somewhere because we left so late, and

I would prefer to get there this evening."

As we started out toward the new road Hamid grew very jovial. I had never seen him in such a happy mood, so completely relaxed. One of his hobbies was designing gardens, and all the way along the road he pointed out different shrubs and plants, describing their characteristics and medicinal properties. Just as we started off onto the new road, he ordered me to stop the car outside a tiny café. Shouting at the people sitting there, he pretended to be very angry, pointing to the ground by their feet and to the wall beside the road. When they looked startled he hit the side of the car with his hand to make the point even clearer, and then told me to drive on.

"What were you doing?" I asked him.

"I told them that they were ignorant fools because they were totally unaware that they were surrounded by a rare herb which kills the parasites that infect everyone here."

He was still laughing a few moments later when we heard a tremendous racket. Coming up behind us was a very old motorcycle. On it were three men, one in front of the other, all shouting and waving their hands, in which they clutched bunches of herbs. I slowed down to let them come up beside us, and then we all stopped by the side of the road. I sat while Hamid listened to what they had to say and then he shouted at them once more, banging his hand on the car several times for emphasis. They all looked very ashamed, climbed back on the motorcycle, and drove off.

"What this time?"

"Oh, the idiots, they brought the wrong herbs. If they had taken those herbs they would have been in the bathroom for a week!"

It was that sort of day. Thus far everything had been light and easy, and even the car seemed happy with the journey. The ominous rattling from the engine had ceased, and although the road was now so steep that we were traveling in second gear, everything seemed fine. Little by little, however, the condition of the road deteriorated until I realized that it wasn't really a road at all. It had started out as a good, fairly flat dirt road, but now it was giving way to what could only be described as a cart track. It was so narrow that even if we had decided to turn around there would have been no chance, and if I were forced to stop the car it was very doubtful that the brakes would hold on the steep incline. I began to get very frightened, and as we rounded each bend the situation grew worse. A rock face rose up on the left, and on the right hand side was a sheer drop of about a thousand feet. Hamid seemed totally unmoved; he sat beside me humming a tune. I did not dare speak to him, as I knew that I should not be afraid. But I was. I was scared stiff. It wasn't just the condition of the car and the road; it was the responsibility. I was driving the car that was carrying the man who was a teacher of the Way, and under the circumstances it seemed certain that any accident would be fatal. I tried in vain to keep my imagination in check.

The road went on and on, and at ten miles an hour in low gear each bend seemed to take an age. By this time the cart tracks were so deep that it was impossible to drive in them for fear of scraping the bottom of the car. It was necessary to drive with two smooth tires on the edge of the cliff and the other two on the raised portion between the tracks. I was shaking, and to make things worse a smell of burning came from the engine. We must be overheating. That would mean that we would have to stop, and I had not brought any water.

As we rounded yet another bend a narrow track joined ours from the left hand side. I caught just a glimpse of something running toward us before I slammed on what brakes we had. A young camel dashed straight toward us, bumped glancingly into the front of the car, hesitated for a second, and then ran on down the track up which we had come. I was drenched with sweat and shaking uncontrollably; I had lost my nerve completely. "Why have you stopped?" Hamid asked sharply. "Drive on. It's getting late, and the lights of the car are very dim."

I simply could not move. I had both feet on the brake and

both hands holding onto the piece of wire that served for a hand brake. The engine was steaming up through the hood, and I had never in my life been so desperate. What was a camel doing up here in the mountains anyway, and where had it come from? "Do you not realize that there is no such thing as chance?" Hamid spoke sharply. "Camels don't live up here, and this one was running straight at us. If you had not reacted quickly in the way you did it would have knocked us over the precipice. Will you please stop shaking and drive on. There may be other animals on this mountain, but that one wasn't really a camel at all."

"But it was a camel," I protested. "We both saw it."

"How do you know, you idiot? You saw a camel, but it was a pretty strange camel to behave in the way it did, don't you think?"

"What do you mean, Hamid?" By this time I was almost crying in frustration and fear, and unable even to change my position in case the car should roll back down the hill.

"I mean that that was a camel, and it was not a camel. Now will you please pull yourself together and drive on up the mountain before I get really angry."

I made one final effort and at last managed to get the car moving. The road seemed to go on and on. Hamid was singing again, but I was still shivering at our narrow escape.

The sun was just going down as we reached the top of the mountain. The view across the plains of Anatolia was breathtaking, but the light was fading and there was no time to stop. It was a long way down, and the road was no better. God only knew where it was leading us anyway. Obviously the man in the café had not known what he was saying when he told us to take this route. The thought went through my mind that perhaps we would end up sleeping by the side of the car and as evening approached it was growing bitterly cold. At that moment Hamid told me to stop the car.

"But we ought to go on," I said. "It's getting dark."

"It is necessary that we stop," he announced. "Nature calls."

He disappeared into the bushes and some time later emerged, singing away to himself as though nothing had happened, as though everything was just as it ought to be. "Drive on," he said as he got back into the car.

On the way down the hill his mood started to change. First he stopped singing and then he became very silent. I tried to talk to him and to question him further about the camel, but he would not speak, and stared stonily at the road in front of him. When the mule track once again began to resemble a road, we were at the bottom of the mountain. Ahead of us stretched a long, perfectly straight road, newly tarmacked. A sign informed us that we were only fourteen kilometers from the place we had set out for that morning.

"We've made it!" I shouted, and at that moment there was a tremendous crunch beneath the car and we ground to a halt. Hamid did not move. He remained sitting impassively, looking straight ahead. Getting out, I looked under the car. The road was covered with oil and a steady stream flowed out of the oil pan. "I'm afraid we've hit a rock and cracked the pan," I said. "Now what do we do?"

"You will wait until another car comes along and then you will arrange for our car to be taken to the nearest town. There was no rock on the road."

"But there must have been! I heard the car hit something."

"Then where is it? If you can find it, show it to me."

Searching all around the car I found no sign of any stone or rock. The road was perfectly smooth, and the edges were of fine gravel.

"Well?" he said from inside the car. "And what is your explanation?"

"Perhaps something happened in the engine," I tried.

"Nothing happened in the engine. There was no rock. You have failed totally and now we are stuck out here with night coming on. Can you remember *nothing?*" On the word "nothing" he turned and glared at me. I was speechless. I could not understand what he was talking about. There *must* have been a rock in the road. I tried to think where I had failed.

"You have come all the way out here to Anatolia. You asked me in England if I would help you, and I told you that it was a dangerous road and that if you did not trust, then we would both falter. Every hour since you have been here I have asked you to trust. Trust. Trust. And what do you do? First you fail totally in the test of courage and behave like an overgrown schoolboy, slobbering as you were on the mountain, and then, without even noticing that you had failed, you announced that you had succeeded when you got to the bottom. As if you could succeed in anything. You, my friend, are nothing, and the sooner you realize it, the sooner you may be able to have some understanding of what this path is about. Who do you think the man in the café was? Do you think that it was just a chance meeting, or that he led us astray by accident? I have told you that there is no such thing as chance. He was not what he appeared to be, any more than the camel was. That man was not an ordinary man, and you were too asleep even to notice."

"You mean you knew it all along?"

"Of course I did, but I have taken on the role, for this short period of time, of being your guide and teacher, and so I had to accept what was sent to you for a test. I didn't know exactly what would happen, but whatever was to come had to be accepted. As it is, you failed every inch of the way. When will you learn to believe in God? You told me you wanted the Truth, yet what you really want is the truth without love. God is Love, and without love there is nothing. If you do not believe in God you will not be able to come to the Truth. You cannot bypass God and think that you will get there by yourself. That is the worst kind of arrogance. Obviously you are going to have to learn humility before we can do any more work together. I must have overestimated you, and I too have failed in my mission if this is the way you behave. Now get out in the road and try to find a car."

I was struck dumb. I felt as though I had been physically

assaulted. I crossed over to the other side of the road and glanced back at the car. Hamid was sitting absolutely straight and still, his eyes closed. No cars passed, no trucks—nothing. I was shaking with anger and with the bitter cold. Hamid thought he had made a mistake, and I was quite sure that I had. I would never have chosen a teacher who behaved like this, and no matter what he said there must have been a stone on the road. I was sick of the whole thing, and I wished that I had never set out on the journey. How could I have been so stupid as to be conned into following this man all the way to Turkey? Who was he, anyway, and what did he want with me? For the moment, I was trapped, but as soon as possible I would get the hell out of this mess, and out of this country, right back to London.

The sound of an engine interrupted my silent tirade. It didn't sound like a car or a truck, but it was definitely approaching. There was no light, so I stood out in the middle of the road. Round the bend came an old tractor. I waved the driver to a halt and pointed to our car, explaining in sign language that it was broken and could he possibly tow us to the nearest town. Looking at me very seriously, he got down off the tractor and walked slowly around the car. Hamid remained sitting bolt upright with his eyes closed. "Hamid," I called, "I have found a tractor. Could you speak with the man, please?"

"Speak to him yourself," was the reply.

Trying to make myself understood was very difficult; the tractor driver continued to circle the car, staring as though it were from another planet. He looked round it, in it, examined the tires and the bumpers, and lifted up the hood. *"Yok,"* he said, which means "no" in Turkish. "But no what?" I asked. "Auto yok," he said firmly. "I know it is yok," I said, "that's why we want you to tow us," and I made all sorts of signs at the front of the car, pretending that I had a rope over my shoulder and was pulling the car along. He did not seem to be impressed and said "yok" several more times. Then he came up very close to me, his breath stinking of garlic, and said fervently, *"Lira, choc lira."* This meant that it was going to cost a lot of money, but I was not sure whether he meant that it would cost a lot to get the car fixed, or whether he wanted a lot to tow us. I asked him how much, and he spelled out an impossibly high figure, drawing with his finger in the oil on the road. I turned to Hamid once more.

"You must pay it," he announced. "There is no point in bargaining, as we are in his hands."

"But it is nearly all the money I have with me."

"You will pay it, and what is more you will also pay for fixing the car, since it is your fault that all this has happened. Now I am tired and hungry and extremely angry. Pay what he asks and hurry up."

Some hours later the car was left outside a small workshop in the village, and we had found one cramped, dirty, and airless room in the local inn. The cost of getting the car fixed was ridiculously high, and Hamid said not another word to me as we made a dreary meal of provisions from the car. There was one large double bed in the room upon which he and I lay down in our clothes. Just as I was drifting off to sleep Hamid shook my shoulder roughly. "Remember," he said, "there was no rock there. If you had not shouted out in that stupid way, 'We've made it,' we might still have proceeded smoothly. Now before you go to sleep pray to be forgiven for your arrogance and carelessness. Otherwise our journey is at an end." With that he rolled over and was soon snoring, the whole bed shaking to the vibration.

The garage man told us in the morning that it would take at least a day to fix the car, as they had to find some spare parts in another town before work could be started, and the car that would collect the parts was away at a wedding in yet another village. The wedding-goers had been due back the day before, we were informed, but it must have been a very good wedding, since no one had yet returned from it. I sat and watched as Hamid addressed the crowd that had begun to gather outside the garage. I could not make out what they were discussing, but I was becoming accustomed to Hamid's ways. It didn't really matter what he said, if anyone was prepared to listen with an inner ear. His words carried deeper meanings than appeared on the surface. I would watch him talking about some sentence from the Koran, or from the writings of one of the Sufi masters, and each of his listeners would get from the discussion as much as they could absorb, no more and no less. At times he would go on and on discussing one particular phrase, and then I would realize that all the energy in the conversation was being directed to one person who was listening correctly.

For my part, I was still shaken by the experiences of the day before. I was bitter and angry, but I also felt that to give up at this stage was pointless and would indicate a marked lack of perseverance. Once, a long time before, Hamid had told me, "To be on this path you need two legs. One is the leg of your predisposition, or the possibilities latent within you, and the other is the leg of perseverance. One without the other is useless."

It had become clear to me that if I were to proceed I would have to give up all of the "knowledge" I thought I had acquired over the years. These three days had completely shattered any aspirations I had had to be a teacher myself. I realized that I knew absolutely nothing. During one of our first meetings in London, Hamid had said to me that if we truly commit ourselves to this path then we are given exactly what we need. Yet did I really need all that I had experienced during this short time? Surely there must be some other way of proving my courage than that drive across the mountains; nothing could persuade me that there had not been a rock lying in the road. I also found it disturbing that, after all this time, Hamid remained such an enigma. I really knew nothing about him at all. It was as though the situation had been taken out of my hands a long time ago and all that had come to pass was unavoidable. I was still struggling with that idea. It was one thing to sense the inevitability of something; it was another to abandon yourself to what was going on. It is easy to know intellectually that it is necessary to go to a teacher with both hands, but actually suspending judgment is very difficult.

As the morning wore on I calmed down and determined to try to trust more. There was nothing to do, so I went for a walk up in the hills behind the village. Everything was still and quiet at noontime. The call to prayer had sounded, and most of the village was deserted. Looking down I could see the square outside the garage and the old car parked by the side of the road. The inn was round the corner of the street, behind some other buildings. Something about this perspective on the quiet dusty town brought back a time when Hamid had talked about the idea of reversing space.

He had explained to me that the average human being believes that he or she is cause to something, and therefore everything starts with the ego center projecting itself outwards onto the screen of life. As long as we live in that space of the ego center, there can be the apparency of change but no real change can come about. It was hard for me to see what real change could mean. He had said that it was not a matter of the expansion of consciousness, but rather of breaking through consciousness. In order to break through consciousness, you must first come upon your true identity. This means leaving behind all concepts, all ideas, all thoughts of what you might be. You must die to what you think you are and be born into what you really are; that is the true heritage of the soul.

Hamid had also told me about another way of viewing life, by allowing oneself to be viewed. He described a spiral moving toward a central point. "What you are," he said, "is the composite manifestation of a moment of time. This spiral is continuously working its way toward the center, re-forming you each moment. But because you think that you are the cause of something, the movement of the spiral is blocked. God needs man, but He can only bring man to Himself when man truly knows that he needs God."

He then taught me an exercise for what he called "reversing space," which involved sitting very still, with all attention focussed in the center of the chest, and slowly surrendering and realizing that instead of looking you are being observed; instead of hearing you are being heard; instead of touching you are being touched; instead of tasting you are food for God and are being tasted. "So make yourself good tasting!" he said. "Finally, allow yourself to be breathed. Abandon yourself completely in trust, and in the realization that you are powerless in the face of God, the First Cause."

I sat there on the hill looking back over the past few days, and I realized that I had ceased to search, and had begun to listen for the answer. I suddenly understood that it is most certainly necessary to seek, to ask the question; rather than pushing away the answer by chasing after it, one must ask and listen at the same time, in trust and good faith that the answer is contained in the question. At that moment I knew that I was being observed, that I was being heard, that I was dissolving and becoming food for the great transformation process that was taking place in the universe. I was no more centered in a place from which everything began with the "little I," but rather the "I" was being formed in me. At the same time that I was dying I was being born, and the senses that I used to hear with, to see with, to taste and touch with, were the senses of a greater Being, used for a purpose that no human mind could comprehend. I was only a vehicle through which something of natural order was being born. There was no need to question or doubt, for in that moment was something that was beyond even trust.

I do not remember how long I remained sitting on the hill; when at last I returned to the village I was very quiet. Hamid obviously knew what was going on, and he did not bother me more than to say that the car would be fixed in the morning and then we would be proceeding. His anger seemed to have gone, and he was busy talking to the mechanic and his friends who had gathered round. The foreign sounds carried intensity but not meaning, and my mind turned to the woman with the blue wool. As I pictured her waiting in her room in

Sidé, sitting beside the window, I felt that I was able to see her for the first time. I allowed her to see me, to look at me and through me. And I began slowly to understand the pain of all women, of the earth, waiting to be recognized so that they can, at last, be free. No more did I see her as a person wounded on the path, but as a living sacrifice to remind the world of the responsibility we have to woman and to the woman within—the unrecognized soul waiting to be born into freedom. She became for me, during those moments, a mirror in which I could see the reflection of the woman within my own being, and the damage that I did her with each moment of forgetfulness.

Hamid interrupted my reverie. I began to tell him my thoughts but he took my arm. "Now you have seen a little, and have been granted a taste of what is to come. One day you will know why she carries the blue wool, and then you will see that the hottest part of the flame, the blue of the flame, is within the center of the fire.

"Tomorrow we will drive on. Plans have changed now, and so we will go to Ephesus to visit Mary. We can get there in a day if we start early, and still have time to prepare ourselves before going up to her chapel."

By the next morning the car had been fixed, and we breakfasted once again on bread and coffee, sitting on the balcony of the little inn.

"Today we begin the next stage of our journey. We are going to visit the place where the Virgin Mary went to live after the crucifixion. There is a chapel there, and normally I ask people to visit Mary on their way down to work with me. For you, however, it was different. I had to see if you would be received by those to whom I sent you in Istanbul and Ankara before I could plan the next steps for you." He looked at me inquiringly. "Is it hard for you to understand these things?"

His question caught me off guard; I thought a moment. "I can't tell you if it's hard or not," I said finally. "The idea of a journey is so new to me. We don't make pilgrimages in England anymore. People may go to Lourdes, but that's different. We don't visit tombs—that sort of thing is considered superstitious. In fact, until I met you the whole idea of God didn't mean very much to me."

"But you believed in Christ, I suppose?"

"I don't know, really. I believe that there was once a great Master called Jesus Christ, but the Spirit of Christ seems to have been lost. I have longed for a taste of the Spirit; maybe that's how I came to take this journey."

"So why all this searching for the Dervishes?" Hamid smiled and looked at me over the top of his glasses. "If you wanted to find the Spirit, which is Christ, what made you travel half way round the world trying to find Dervishes in Turkey?"

"Well, you see, I felt that there was some hidden knowledge that the Dervishes had which would help me. . . ." Even as I said it I realized that it was not really true at all. It dawned on me that I had never really sat down to consider why I was chasing after these people. It had seemed unavoidable, but Hamid's questions made me wonder if there was a need to find them after all. What was I really looking for?

"Let me tell you a little about the inner meaning of the Virgin Mary before we arrive at her chapel." Hamid seemed determined to push me into some sort of realization.

"You must first of all understand that although I seem to be talking about an historical event, everything of which I speak is within you and is happening at *this moment.* There is no other; and what happened, in our world, two thousand years ago is part of the unfoldment of this moment, not *that* moment but this very instant. It is neither a question of looking back two thousand years nor of trying to recapture the moment in your imagination. All you have to do is to be awake. Be awake in this moment within yourself, and it will be your own understanding. It may take time to unfold in our world, but the Truth, and the unfoldment of the Truth, is always there."

He paused, and was silent for so long that my mind began to wander—to the remains of our breakfast, to the proposed trip to Ephesus, to the state of repair of the car. Finally he leaned forward in his chair and looked at me searchingly. "I want you to listen to me carefully," he said. "Make your mind quiet and just listen.

"Your body is the Virgin Mary. The Spirit is Christ, the Word that was conveyed through Gabriel the eternal messenger. The breath is the Breath of the Mercy of God, and it is that breath that quickens the soul. Until the soul is quickened by the Spirit it is like an unfledged bird.

"There are many paths to God, but the way of Mary is the sweetest and most gentle. If you can melt into Mary, the matrix, the blueprint of life, the Divine Mother, you will be formed and shaped in Christ and Christ in you, and thus through the breath of God's Mercy you will come into being and know Him. For it is the breath of mercy that bestows being. Every moment God appears in living form, never manifesting himself twice in the same moment.

"Mary brought Jesus into the world because she was chosen to be the one for this work, and so she was trained in the knowledge of birth. It is said that Gabriel, the messenger, appeared to Mary in the form of a man. She thought that he wanted her as a woman, so she froze for a moment, turning to her Lord. If she had not relaxed, then the child born from that moment would have been uncompromising and impossible to live with. Your body is the Virgin Mary, the Spirit is Christ, the breath is the breath of God's Mercy. Your soul remains asleep until it is quickened by the Holy Spirit. Each moment of our lives a child is born somewhere. The child that is born could be a God-conscious human being, or it could be uncompromising, in endless competition with life. The responsibility in the realization of these things is immense. If you can hear what I am saying to you now, then you will begin to understand. As you are permeated with the Spirit, you may, Insh'allah, begin to know, but it will not make life easier or lighter for you. It may make life heavier, but heavier with meaning and purpose.

"Mary is the Divine Mother. Mary is in the blue of the flame, and Mary is the matrix of all divine possibility in form, here, in our world. It is necessary that she be recognized. Learn to love God with all of your being, every part of yourself, your heart, your mind, your soul, and then we may all be granted the understanding of the meaning of the virgin birth. Learn to pray and your prayers will come back from the very matrix that forms the child.

"A Sufi is called 'the son of the moment.' As you melt each moment into Mary, something is being redeemed that a child may be born, and what is being born is the son of the moment. That child may become God-realized and thus be called a Sufi, or he may walk the earth unaware, asleep—not yet human, not conscious of God or of the wonders of His creation, having no knowledge of himself and thus no real understanding of love. Your body is the Virgin Mary—remember this each moment of your life. This is the responsibility that we must take as we come into knowledge, into being.

"Mary was chosen to bear Jesus because she kept her purity intact. Simple people call this her 'virginity,' but those who know understand that to be pure means to be completely adaptable, to flow with each moment, to be like a running stream cascading from the waters of life itself. To be pure is to spread joy, and joy is the unfoldment of the knowledge of the perfection of God. The 'Work' that you have been searching for is the Spirit of God, and the Spirit of God is the Christ which comes to redeem the world. The eternal messenger is always within, waiting to unfold the moment through the Word, and one day when Mary is recognized again, there will be a reappearance of the Christ, manifested in the outer world. Remember who Mary is, and one day, when you are ready, and when God so wills it, you will know what I have told you."

Most of that day we drove in silence. Although I could remember the words that Hamid had spoken to me that morning, and had been able to put them down in my notebook, I knew that it might be many years before I could understand their true content. I remember feeling humbled and ashamed that I had once more underestimated what Hamid was teaching me. Somehow my search for the Dervishes seemed meaningless now; in fact, much of my search seemed to have been a waste of time. A desire was growing in me to know just what was behind this whole journey, to understand all the stepping stones on the path to this moment.

"We will not stop at the town of Ephesus now," Hamid told me. "It's late already and we must go to Mary before sundown. Perhaps we will stay the night and look round the city tomorrow. The best way to go to her is to walk the six kilometers up the hill, but I am tired now. When you come back, though, then you must walk."

The road up the mountain was steep, with many hairpin bends, and a spectacular view of the countryside. Nothing much has changed there since the time of the crucifixion, except for the tarmacked roads and the busloads of tourists. Shepherds and goatherds walk the hills with their flocks, the terraces of gray-green olive trees have born fruit since the beginning of history, and the clothes worn by the men and women in the fields are the same as they have always been. It was as though we were driving into a Biblical scene that would remain just as it was until the end of time.

We parked the car at the top of the hill and walked toward the chapel. The tourist restaurants and gift shops took away some of the magic at first, but then the noise of the tourists died down and we turned a corner to find a Mass being held in the open air. An altar had been set out, and perhaps a hundred people were kneeling on the ground. There were dark-skinned Turks from the East and women in rough black dresses and pilgrims from Istanbul and Europe. A sense of deep peace and inner quiet was everywhere and I longed to kneel with the others. "Come," said Hamid, "first to Mary."

Her chapel was a very small stone building surrounded by

huge trees. The inside of the chapel was cool and shadowy, lit by hundreds of flickering candles, each one an offering of love. We bought candles at the door and lit them, placing them carefully in the niches which lined the walls.

Hamid stood before the altar and prayed. Following him, I asked to understand the purpose of this journey into the unknown, and prayed to be led to the Truth.

We did not stay long at the chapel, but walked to one of the nearby cafés for coffee. "Perhaps you wonder how it is that I can pray to God through Mary, even though I was brought up in the Moslem faith," Hamid said as we sat down. "Did you know that in every mosque there is a prayer niche dedicated to Mary? We are not involved with the form of religion. We are concerned with the truths that lie silent, waiting to be revealed, within all religions. Once you know, then in your love of God you pay respects to all His Messengers. Some of the Messengers are known, some will never be known.

"Today marks the beginning of a new life for you—that is, if you have been humble enough, and if you have truly come with both hands, leaving everything behind you. Mary receives only those who come with all of their being. It is the same as the eye of the needle that you talk about. To get through the eye of the needle you have to lose your opinions, realizing that you know nothing. To be received by Mary, it is necessary that you melt.

"In the tradition of Islam, everything starts with the acceptance of the Unity of God, that there is just One Absolute Being from which all stems, and within which all exists. I can say that I believe in the virgin birth because I understand the things that we have been talking about; I look at the inner meaning of the words, and am not caught in the world of form.

"But we have said enough for now. It is getting late, so we will stay for the night and have a meal in a wonderful restaurant I know of, and drive on in the morning."

That evening I sat on the edge of my bed in the hotel room

in Ephesus and pondered what I had heard that day. Hamid had gone to his room, saying that he wanted to be alone after his visit to Mary. I felt the same need, and was grateful for the opportunity to just sit quietly by myself.

My meditation was interrupted some time later by Hamid's footsteps as he paced the floor of his room, which was above mine. He had seemed very nervous before going to his room; now I could hear him walking, walking, and I wondered if something was wrong. Suddenly I heard a crash upstairs, and the sound of breaking crockery, as though he had thrown a large object across the room and had broken a pile of plates and glasses. I ran upstairs, taking three steps at a time, and banged on his door. There was no immediate answer, and then I heard him say, "Come in." He was standing in the center of the room. On the table by the window a glass vase lay broken, and his suitcase was lying open on the floor, the clothes scattered all around. He held his glasses in his hand, and one of the lenses was shattered.

"I heard a crash," I said. "Is everything all right?"

"No, it isn't. Something is wrong. We must go back to Sidé immediately. Get your things together and we will leave as soon as possible."

"But Hamid," I protested, "we have hardly any lights, and it's dark and it's going to take us all night to get there."

"What has that got to do with it? How many more times must I tell you to trust. There is something not right. I don't yet know what it is, but we must return at once."

"But how do you know?" I asked, bewildered.

"Enough! Get your case and come. And pay the bill on the way out." Then he bundled all his clothes together, stuffing them into the suitcase, and hurried down the stairs.

As soon as I could I joined him in the car. It was quite dark and the stars filled the sky. I noticed that there was a half moon.

All night we drove. Hamid never said a word. He either sat there staring out the front of the car or else he leaned back and slept, snoring loudly. The lights of the car were so dim that it required every ounce of concentration to stay on the road. Since it was not the tourist season, there were few cars, and as dawn broke we were within a hundred kilometers of Antalya.

"Drive straight to Sidé," Hamid said. "Have you enough gas?"

"I don't think so—it's very low."

"Never mind, we must trust—there is no time to waste."

I drove the last twenty kilometers with the needle showing zero. We did not run out of gas, though, and reached the house just as the village began to wake.

Not waiting for the car to be parked, Hamid told me to stop outside the door. He climbed out quickly, and as he did so he hit his head on the side of the door, knocking off his glasses. I ran around to pick them up and handed them to him. "The glasses are not important," he said. "Come quickly."

We entered the house. I had no idea what to expect; nothing seemed to be out of order. Hamid ran around the house, and then across the courtyard to the girl's room, below my own. He knocked on the door but there was no answer. "Go and look in your room," he ordered.

"For what?" I asked.

"There must be something there. Go quickly and see."

I ran upstairs and into the room. She was sitting on the side of the bed. The blue wool was everywhere, on the bed, caught round the bedpost, and spreading out onto the floor. Her hair was dishevelled and her eyes blazed with tremendous anger. She looked at me and pointed with both hands at an envelope on the floor. Picking it up, I saw that it was addressed to me in care of Hamid. I called down to him, and he came hurrying up the stairs. "Open it," he said, hardly even bothering to look at the girl who got up to greet him.

It was a telegram from my business partner, short and straight to the point. "Return at once," it began. "Your attention urgent re sale of business. . . ."

"You stupid idiot!" Hamid shouted. "You said that you

would come with both hands and that you would leave nothing behind. Now I know why things have been so difficult. Just get out. Go back, and do what you have to do."

With that he left the room. The girl sat there, her huge eyes fixed on me. She could hardly have understood what had been said. "Come on," I said to her, "let's go down to your room." I led her down the stairs; she carried the pile of wool carefully in both hands. I opened the door with one hand, holding on to her with the other, and led her to the chair by the desk. She was crying silently now, huge tears pouring down her face.

"I must go to England," I said. "There are things that I have to do, but I will come back as soon as I can. We can talk then?" She did not respond. I ran back up the stairs to my room and began to pack.

seven

What you are looking for is what is looking.
—St. Francis of Assisi

I said, "Thou art harsh, like such a one."
"Know," he replied,
"That I am harsh for good, not from rancor and spite.
Whoever enters saying, "Tis I," I smite him on the brow;
For this is the shrine of Love, O fool! it is not a sheep cote!
Rub thine eyes, and behold the image of the heart."
—Mevlana Jelalu'ddin Rumi

"But, Hamid, I had to go back. Sometimes these things happen and plans have to be changed. It's all fixed now, though—there isn't anything else to interfere with my commitment here. I've put everything in the hands of an attorney and told him that I will be out of England for an indefinite period, and he has complete authority to sign papers for me, and all that sort of thing."

Since I had returned to Sidé, Hamid had hardly spoken. I had been away for just under a week and had returned as quickly as I could, having sent a telegram from London to announce that the business problems had been settled and that I would soon be back with him. Then, after three days of silence, he responded to my pleading and explanations.

"You swore that you had left nothing behind. I told you that it was not possible for us to go on this journey together unless you came with both hands. It seems that the time is not right and it is better for you to go back to England, get a normal job, and then ask me again in another year when you are more prepared."

"Please, Hamid," I begged. "Really it's all right now and there is nothing to take me away again. There is nothing more important than this time. I know that."

"Now you listen to me carefully." Hamid sat up straight in his chair, slamming his fist on the table. "You are the most stubborn and obstinate person I have ever met. You simply do not listen to what you are being told. You don't seem to care, even after all your so-called searching, about the importance of true work on yourself. You think you have a right to an opinion. You have no right even to think that you know. If you want to understand the Way, then you have to make sacrifices. But do you? Do you really make any sacrifices? Perhaps you've given up a little of your comfort, and some of your British conditioning, but to truly come to understand you have to sacrifice *everything*. If you had really done this, you would not have been called back to London for a ridiculous business talk which was quite unnecessary. 'You cannot serve God and mammon,' isn't that what you say?"

"Why are you so angry, Hamid?" I asked him. "Why is one week so important? It's not as though I hadn't come right back. And if I hadn't gone to London then, most likely I would have been called back for a much longer period later on."

"How do you know?" he shouted at me. "What do you know about that? You still won't hear what I am telling you. Trust, trust, trust! If you had come with both hands, and trusted in God, then do you really think this could have happened? You know that there is no such thing as chance. So listen to me and I'll tell you the real reason you were called back to England.

"The moment you set foot on this path there is no turning back. But you became complacent after you arrived here. I have watched you. In your pride and arrogance you thought you were achieving something. There is nothing to achieve, there is only surrender to a life of service. But you have gone on spiritualizing your ego, always tied up in your opinions and your concepts. The goal of this journey is far beyond anything you can conceive of.

"You thought it was mere coincidence or perhaps even because of stupidity on the part of your business partner that you were called back to London. But that is not so. Instead of giving up totally and trusting in God, you kept just a little of what you thought could buy you comfort back in London. Is that not so?"

At that moment I wanted more than anything else never to have begun this journey. I felt ashamed. I knew that what he was saying was true. I had left things in a way that allowed me a sort of insurance policy, so that I could still return to the old life as though nothing had happened. After I had made these arrangements, I had put them completely out of my mind, but it was clear that when my partner had summoned me back to help him deal with thc problems involved in selling our antique business, he had simply played a part in exposing my own lack of faith.

"Now listen to me. I'm not interested in your self-pity, and what's more, I'm not through with you yet. There is another reason why I was so upset when you went back to England. It was a very important sequence of events that led us both to Mary at Ephesus. It was then you were initiated into the beginnings of the inner path that is the foundation of what I have been trying to convey to you. Once you have been introduced into that path it is necessary that you work twice as hard on yourself so that you can be taken on to the next stage of the unfoldment of the mystery. Just when that unfoldment was beginning for you, you went running off to England, completely breaking the continuity of our work together. And it was only because of your unwillingness to sacrifice your security that you had to go back at all. That is why you must not leave anything behind—for it is certain that any unfinished business will prevent you from taking the next step toward full commitment. Now that you have come back, you must reaffirm your commitment if we are to continue together."

He was silent briefly, as though considering how to proceed. "If you really say 'I will,' in consciousness, to the Will of God, then I pity you, for I know of the sacrifices that you will have to make before you may be granted the knowledge of our essential Unity with God.

"If you want to come upon that Truth, you must learn to rededicate yourself with every breath you draw, turn to God with every step. Each morning, as you wake, you should pray that you will be allowed to be of service, asking nothing for yourself in return.

"Now you must decide if you are really ready to go on, to dedicate yourself unconditionally to the Work of God on Earth."

I felt closer to Hamid than ever before, and more able to trust. "Yes," I said, "I will."

Hamid stood up and embraced me as though I were his son. "I am glad you have come back," he said. "I have missed you very much."

We were both crying now, and the flow of love between us washed away what was past.

"Thank you," I said, "thank you for taking me back, and being patient with me."

"When you know," he said, smiling, "you will say 'Thank you' each moment, for each moment is, in essence, perfect. Indeed, His ways are beautiful. I'm sorry to be so hard on you sometimes, but I'm afraid some people have to learn the hard way.

"Now we will rest, and tomorrow morning you will come to me as usual and we will see what is to be done next.

"Also, you should know that the girl disappeared the day you left for England. I didn't tell you sooner because until I decided to accept you again, it was none of your business. I heard that she got a ride to Antalya, but no one seems to have seen her. I have checked all the hotels and asked all the travel agents, but so far there's no sign of her. She has done this before, but you should remember her in your prayers. She wants so much to be helped."

We went for a walk along the beach the next morning instead of having the usual session in his room. We walked in silence toward the amphitheater. In the last day I had been brought close to what Hamid called the state of perplexity, the point at which we finally turn to God and discover that all our self-importance is illusion. Despair had come when I realized that I knew nothing at all, that I was incapable of acting even to help bring about the change that was necessary in myself. Yet Hamid had also told me that it is at the very moment we realize our impotence that we draw near the beginning of the path of knowledge.

We sat down by the rocks facing the ocean. Hamid was still silent, but as so often his silence carried more intensity than his words. It seemed that every moment was precious to him, and the depth of his feelings gave an added dimension to every action and experience that we shared. The more we were together the less time made any sense to me, and space had been swallowed up in the traveling to and from London and Istanbul. The invisible structure of time that allows us to experience distance was dissolving and there were moments when I felt great fear as I realized that there was less and less to hang on to, fewer and fewer props to keep alive the illusions that I had treasured.

Hamid stood up on the rock where we were sitting, raising his arm to point out the great curve of the bay. It was a perfect morning. The cold wind had died down, and the sun was bright and clear, making the sea shine and sparkle. It was very quiet; I could just hear the creaking of the oars of a fishing boat by the rocks off the point.

"Is it not beautiful?" he asked me. "The sole purpose of love is beauty. Living should be an act of love. Fill everyone around you with the freedom of that spirit. Never be controlled by your passions, but dare to live passionately. For until you come to love completely you will never come to know God!

"But now tell me, what have you really understood so far since you and I have been together? Not with the mind, but with the heart?"

I dreaded these questions. It was hard enough letting go of my old concepts, but it was harder still trying to put into words those small realizations that I could truthfully say I understood.

"I think the most important thing," I began, "is that what I had thought I had understood from previous teachings was not real. There were moments, flashes of inspiration, but most of the time I was just gathering together masses of information which now seem to be useless."

Hamid smiled. "It's not that bad, is it?" he asked.

"I don't know. Last night I was nearly in despair, for when you said that really there was nothing to achieve, all my past life seemed pointless, just a great waste of time. I don't feel happy any more. I don't know what I feel."

"The reason for that," he replied, "is simple. As your conditioning goes so do your habit patterns, and then comes a period when everything can seem very negative. Don't worry about it. If you did not experience such things, I would know that you were refusing to give up some of the most treasured possessions of your mind. Always there is a sense of loss as the illusions go, but it is a temporary state and will pass. Go on, what else can you tell me?"

"Well, when I was in London I found that I could hardly speak with anyone, even my oldest friends. They seemed very suspicious, and the more I tried to tell them what had been going on, the worse it became. I found that I simply could not communicate the things we've been doing here. It was a great shock, and I felt that I had failed them in some way, because they have always wanted the same things that I did."

"Ah," said Hamid, "but I tell you—your job is to create a new language. You do not understand this yet. When your heart finally opens, you will be able to speak from the heart, and they will understand what you are saying. Remember, however, that we each understand in our individual ways, not necessarily in the form that you are trying to communicate."

"How will I know when this is happening? How do I tell when I'm really speaking from the heart?"

"That is not an easy question to answer, since if your heart were opened, you would know. But I can say this. If you speak with this new language, then you will see real change coming about in the people with whom you are trying to communicate. The word, together with the breath, carries the Spirit into the relative world and brings about this change. Without real change there is no freedom, either for the seeker on the path or for those with whom he comes in contact.

"You see, the heart is the seat of the soul. When you speak from the heart you can kindle the fire in the hearts of others. Through recognition you actually begin to awaken the soul which is asleep. And fire spreads—there is nothing more catching than love.

"But first you have to die in love if you wish to live as a real human being and thus bring others to love. That is why it is said in Islam, 'Die before you die.' We have to learn to die to each moment; and as we die in love so we are re-formed in love.

"It needs great courage to die each moment. But until you can truly surrender you are not yet a *salik,* a traveler on the Way. A salik is one who has found himself. And when he knows himself he knows the truth, and knows what needs to be done. He sees from the vantage point of knowledge itself and so contributes toward the change that is necessary. He understands that God needs man's sacrifice and surrender so that evolution can proceed.

"We are at a point of history when many of the traditional forms are collapsing. Everyone is frantically trying to shore up the religious, political, and economic forms of the Western way of life. Politicians and economists try one thing after another to bring about stability, but nothing really happens. There is no real change. And you spiritual seekers go all over the world trying to find the answers to your own pain and confusion. You go to gurus in India, and to swamis, astrologers, analysts—all sorts of people whose ways you try for a little while. Now it seems that you are trying the Dervishes!" He smiled knowingly at me.

"But is there real change?" he went on. "What real change do you see? There is still the same confusion, and the deterioration of the old order continues. Everyone is trying to find an answer to the question, but it doesn't matter how much they measure and have opinions—nothing can really happen because people lack the courage to face change. They want methods to placate their self-righteousness, or explanations of phenomena which they can measure—anything but real change. But listen to me! At this time, if real change is not brought about, if people do not become saliks, then there is a very real danger that the earth will revert to a state of primordial chaos. It could be, if enough work is not done at the highest level soon, that we will see the end of civilization in our lifetime. Already we have seen such deterioration that it is questionable just how much can be done."

The intensity of Hamid's words was frightening. I felt that he was trying to express something to me that was of the utmost importance, something that I was not yet willing to face. My rational mind blocked what he was saying.

"You are telling me," I said finally, "that the future of the world, of this planet, depends on us and the real changes that we make now."

"That is exactly what I am telling you," Hamid replied. "We are preparing now for the world to come, but when it will come is in God's time and not in ours. All you can do now is to work harder and harder on yourself, sleep less and pray more that you may be given understanding, and in that way it will be easier for you when the time comes. But the time can only come when you have no past to make your mind spin fruitlessly in its habitual patterns. There are many stages beyond what we have touched on, but I cannot tell you when you will be ready to hear of them. It may be in a week that we will begin. It may be in a month. It may not be for years. It depends on you.

"It is the same with the world. The world is full of concepts and ideas, when what it needs is recognition so that love can melt away all the pain and the conditioning, and man and the invisible worlds can cooperate together to build a new way of life in *this* world. Most of the time you think that I am just talking about you, and that is because you are so completely self-centered that you don't listen properly. Do you not see what this means? If you truly give yourself up, then what I am saying is being said to all those who can hear, and there is no need for us to leave this rock for this to come about. Turn inside out so that you can be of service, and then the words that I speak will be heard by all those in the world who are ready to listen."

All the rest of that morning Hamid was in a jovial mood, insisting that we play patience hour after hour. Each time I tried to bring the conversation around to the earlier talk, he would interrupt and stop me before I could so much as complete a question. When I was sick of playing patience, I asked him if we could play something else.

"Why should you want to play something else?" he asked. "Patience is a game which can bring out a quality that you must learn. Patience is essential, for otherwise you act too quickly and disturb the plan. The seeds must be sown, then you must wait until they come up at the right time. If you go digging about in the earth before they are ready you will destroy what has been planted. Patience is one of the most important qualities for anyone who enters this path. You are far too impatient, and that is why I am playing patience with you."

"But I'm fed up with this game. You jump from one thing to another, then just when I think we're going to get somewhere and follow up a line of thought you're off again on another track and I don't know where I am."

"That," he announced pleasantly, "is exactly what I intend. Now cut the cards, please."

That afternoon we ate a late lunch in the restaurant. The night's catch had been laid out, and we chose a huge plate of different sorts of fish flavored with wild thyme and fennel, which the cook grilled over charcoal. Hamid was in a talkative mood, and the usual crowd gathered while he expounded in Turkish. Two weeks ago I would have been offended that he did not pay attention to me, but now I was content to eat quietly and to enjoy watching the men mending their nets by the beached fishing boats. Something had happened that morning; I was no longer trying to understand, and there was no need to do anything but relax to the sounds of the water and feel the afternoon sun on my face.

After the leisurely meal, we took a nap on the beach. When we awoke, Hamid suddenly announced that I was to go on a journey by myself the next day. It was a jolt after the peaceful afternoon. Also the girl had not yet reappeared, and I had planned to see if I could find out where she had gone when she left Sidé.

"Don't complain," Hamid warned me. "You do not yet know the cause of these things. You are to go tomorrow to Konya to visit three great saints. You should make all the necessary arrangements today. If you ask Mustafa at the restaurant he will get the ticket and arrange for you to have a car to get to the bus terminal."

"But what are you going to do?" I asked him.

"I shall also be traveling tomorrow. A friend of mine is driving me to Istanbul, where I will stay at my cousin's house on the Bosphorous. I will give you the address, and you can join me there."

"But how long should I stay in Konya?"

"That depends on the way in which you go there. The main thing is that you should go with a completely open mind. Do you remember the postcard I gave you in England when I said that you could come to join me?"

I certainly could not have forgotten it, for I had carried it with me to Turkey. I told Hamid that the card was in my suitcase, and that I looked at it often.

"That card is a picture of the tomb of Mevlana Jelalu'ddin Rumi. He is the one to whom you must now go to pay your respects. Mevlana means Our Master, and in our tradition he is known as the Pole of Love. If you go properly and are received, you may learn a great deal from him."

"When did he live?" I asked.

"Mevlana lived in the thirteenth century. I would like to tell you about his life and teachings, but just now I think it is better for you to go on alone. Perhaps when we meet in Istanbul we can talk about him a little.

"There are three places that you must go in Konya, and you must go to them in the proper order. The first one is the tomb of Shams–i Tabriz, the Sun of Tabriz. He was a wandering Dervish who led Mevlana into complete abandonment to God. Then you must visit the tomb of Sadru'ddin Konevi, who was one of Mevlana's earliest and greatest teachers, for he represents the link between Mevlana, who is called the Pole of Love, and Sheikh al-Akbar, Muhyi-d-din Ibn 'Arabi, referred to in our tradition as the Pole of Knowledge. And last you are to go to the tomb and museum of Mevlana. He too wanted everyone to dance." I could not be sure, but I thought Hamid winked at me. "It's a pity that you weren't with me in December, when I was in Konya for the great celebration that is held every year to mark the night of his death, or, as they call it, his 'wedding night,' when he was taken completely into Union.

"But enough for the moment. Now go and make the necessary arrangements, then please come and say good-bye to me in the morning before you leave. I think that the bus leaves from Antalya around six A.M., so you must be up very early."

eight

Make yourself free from self at one stroke!
Like a sword be without trace of soft iron;
Like a steel mirror, scour off all rust with contrition.
—Mevlana Jelalu'ddin Rumi

My existence is from you and your appearance is through Me.
Yet if I had not appeared, you would not have been.
—Muhiy-d-din Ibn 'Arabi

After the south, the long ride to Konya was bitterly cold. The steppes of Anatolia were frozen wastelands, and although it was somewhat warm in the bus, whenever we stopped for rest and refreshment the freezing wind cut into the bus and we would run to the restaurant to take bowls of hot soup and coffee. People were wrapped tightly in sheepskin coats, and the women wore their shawls drawn closely about their heads and necks. Many of the men wore huge fur hats with earflaps against the cold; they stood about in the stations smoking dark Turkish cigarettes. The cold had an effect on the personalities of these people. Missing was the incessant conversation typical of southern Turkey; the passengers just sat in silence, waiting for the bus horn to be sounded. Then we would all climb back into the bus and settle down for the next few hours until the time came to stop once more. Even the old man sitting beside me had only greeted me once, when he sat down at the beginning of the trip. *"Merhaba*—greetings," he had said, and that was all. This was quite different from the other journeys I had taken, when everyone clustered around wanting to know why I was in Turkey and where I was going and what I was going to do.

For some reason I had imagined Konya to be a very primitive town; it was a surprise to find a modern bus station and taxis waiting. We had driven through the outskirts just as the sun was setting. Now the streets were lit and the headlights of the cars reflected off the ice on the sides of the roads. Everyone clambered out of the bus, and all the luggage was laid out to be collected. The peace of the journey dissolved in the excitement of those coming to greet their friends and relatives after the long ride. Once more it was the Middle East, with all the noise and the rush and the excitement of the streets and markets in every town in Turkey.

"You want taxi, sir? Very cheap."

"How much?"

"Very cheap sir, you get in and we go to hotel, yes?"

"But how much?"

"Just twenty-five lira, fixed price always, sir."

"All right," I said, "I will go with you, but twenty-five lira no. I will give you ten lira."

"Not possible, sir, fixed price always."

"Then I will walk," I said, picking up my suitcase and starting off up the street.

"You very hard man, sir, but will give you special price—twenty lira." The taxi driver was running after me trying to take my suitcase away.

"Fifteen," I said, hanging on and walking faster.

"All right, sir, fifteen and some cigarettes."

"I don't smoke," I said, and got into the cab with the feeling of having won a battle. As soon as we set off it was as though there had been no bargaining at all. All the way to the hotel, the taxi driver told me about his family and asked the usual questions—how I liked Turkey, how long I would be in Konya, whether I would like to rent a car from his brother-in-law.

Hamid had given me the address of a hotel in the center of town, near the tomb of Mevlana Jelalu'ddin Rumi. I was greeted by the owner of the hotel, who told me that there was plenty of room as it was not the time of year for tourists to visit Konya. "You are just passing through?" he asked. I told him that I did not know how long I would be staying. He took my bags upstairs to a small room on the second floor, just above the lounge. Handing me the key he left, and I was alone.

I slept late the next morning, exhausted by the long bus trip, and it was almost noon before I was ready to begin my search. The owner of the hotel was very helpful when I told him that I wanted to visit the tomb of Shams–i Tabriz. "I pray for you that the tomb is open today," he said. "Sometimes it is, and sometimes it isn't. But if you are intended to be there, then Allah will provide the key for the door to be opened."

It had never entered my mind that the tomb would be closed, as Hamid had specifically instructed me to see the tombs in order, starting with Shams–i Tabriz. It was quite a shock to find the iron gates shut and the square outside the tomb deserted. A few pigeons were drinking from the fountain; otherwise there was nothing. The door was locked and bolted, and there was no way to see through the window. It was cold, and an icy wind was blowing across the town. I was overcome with sadness. Until that moment all doors had been opened to me; even when I had failed to find the Sheikh in Istanbul, it had not seemed to be a rejection. This was quite a different matter; I was suddenly filled with loneliness. It was illogical, yet the more I tried to battle with the experience the worse it became. I sat down on the edge of the square and tried to compose my thoughts, but nothing seemed to change my mood. That closed door represented for me every time I had been rejected in my life. Surely I had gone properly, with both hands, this time.

I tried to look back over the bus trip to see if I had done anything which would have brought about this situation. By this time I was convinced that nothing happens by chance; therefore the fact that the tomb was closed meant I was being taught something. But I could find nothing that would set my mind at ease. Now what was I to do? There was no one to ask, and there was no notice on the door to say when the tomb would be open.

I must have remained there for half an hour, fighting my depression, before I suddenly realized what was wrong. I had arrogantly presumed that the tomb would be open and I would be received. Although I had thought that I had gone to Konya with all my heart, I had actually gone without any humility at all. So that was it! Obviously I was not to be received because I had forgotten, once again, the proper attitude. I realized in that instant that without humility there is only pain and the sense of separation.

In one way I felt that there was little point in pursuing the visits to the tombs. If it was necessary to go to them in a certain order, it would be better to wait until the next day to see if it were possible then. On the other hand, as there was nothing else to do, I decided to follow my instructions, and to try to find the tomb of Sadru'ddin Konevi, without wasting any more time.

I soon realized that not all of the narrow twisted streets were shown on the map I had brought, and within a few minutes I was quite lost. The map showed that Mevlana's tomb was much closer than that of Konevi, and much easier to find, so I decided to go straight there. I worked my way out of the maze of alleys and there, at the end of the street, was the magnificent tomb and museum of Mevlana. I suddenly realized that the sun was low in the sky. I had spent the entire day in this pilgrimage and had arrived almost by accident at my final destination. Apparently I was meant to visit Mevlana first. I crossed the square quickly and arrived at the gates just as the guard came out to close them. "Sorry, sir, tomb closed today now. Open tomorrow, Insh'allah."

Back in the hotel I lay on my bed, staring at the ceiling, unable to stop the bitterness that overtook me. I fell asleep, finally, and when I awoke it was dark. The lights were on in the streets outside; somehow I had managed to sleep right through to supper time.

I realized that I had been dreaming about Hamid. He was like a mirror, so clearly polished that I had only to look into it to see exactly what was going on at that moment, and thus to come closer to discovering the essence of the moment itself. As the journey unfolded he had guided me carefully into a position in which the search for the Truth had begun to destroy the searcher, so that I no more knew who I was, or who it was that had set out on the journey. It was as though I were slowly turning inside out. What I was looking for was what was looking!

It became clear to me that it is the passionate desire of God that we know the Truth that makes us search, and the Truth is nothing other than Himself. The fire is everywhere in latency, but it is up to us to light the match and kindle the flame in our longing to return to Him. It is we who have to make the first step.

The following morning I tried once again to pay my respects to Shams-i Tabriz. There had been a change in the weather and the ice had turned to slush so that the dirty streets were running mud, the women were picking their way through the puddles, holding their long skirts above their ankles. There was a light drizzle and I was reminded of a typical winter day in London.

Coming around the corner by the square I became aware that someone was following me. I had the definite sense that I was in danger. Yet I was unable either to slow down or to quicken my step. Soon my unknown companion was walking only a pace or so behind me. The tension became worse and worse and was suddenly broken when I felt a hand on my shoulder. Spinning around, I fully expected to be attacked.

I stopped myself just as I was about to hit him. I had seen this man before. Instead of assaulting me, the stranger threw his arms around me and embraced me as though I was a long-lost friend. In the strength of his embrace, and due to the fact that I was half buried in his overcoat, I had no chance to look at his face. He was speaking to me in rapid Turkish, and all I could understand was the word *Döst,* which means "friend" in Persian. Finally he let me go, placed his hand over his heart, and said, "Istanbul, Istanbul." It was the bookseller I had met in Istanbul when I had been looking for the Sheikh. This was truly amazing. What on earth was he doing in the back streets of Konya that morning? We couldn't communicate very well because of the language problem, but this didn't seem to bother him in the slightest. He took me by the arm, talking to me all the time in Turkish, and before I knew what was happening we had arrived in the square of the tomb of Shams–i Tabriz. He walked me quickly to the other side by the iron gates, and then, letting go of my arm, he put his hand on his heart and bowed deeply. I did the same. Then he led me toward the door of the tomb. Once again it was locked. He looked puzzled, and tried the lock carefully. Then he went around to the back of the building, and I heard him talking to someone. Soon he returned and, after several minutes with my Turkish phrase book and dictionary, I gathered that the man who had the key to the tomb was ill and so it would not be opened that day.

This time I did not become depressed. The presence of the bookseller was significant enough, and he seemed as saddened as I was that we could not go inside the building. He made all sorts of apologies, and pointed to the word "tomorrow" in my Turkish-English dictionary. In the meantime, he indicated, I was to go with him. His manner made it more of an order than an invitation, so I followed obediently as he hurried through the streets. We walked for a long time in the drizzling rain, until we arrived at a small block of apartments. Beckoning to me to follow, he went upstairs to the second floor. Outside the door was a pile of shoes, and he pointed to mine as he took off his own. I did the same, and then he knocked. The door was opened a crack and a woman's face peered out at us. "Ah," she said. The chain was undone and the door opened.

Everything had happened so fast that I had not had time to think, but somehow it was not a surprise to find that the room was jammed with about forty men ranging in age from the late teens to one very old man, bent almost double, who might have been ninety years old. The bookseller beckoned to me, and a space was made for me on the sofa. Pointing around the room, he smiled, saying, "Dervish, Dervish," then he was shown to a large chair standing by itself at one end of the room. As he sat down all the others in the room bowed, touching their foreheads to the floor. He began to chant, his voice oddly thin and nasal. The loud response from the men in the room was a strange contrast. I could not understand the words he was chanting, but at the end of each line they all responded, "Hu-Allah, Hu-Allah." Soon a very large tambourine was produced and some of the Dervishes began a rhythmic clapping, their bodies swaying in time with the music. The two men on either side of me took my hands in theirs. There was no time to stop and question what was going on. I was transported into the rhythm, and soon found myself joining in with the responses. The rhythm grew stronger and faster and by now all the Dervishes were holding hands and swaying back and forth. Those who had been sitting on the chairs and sofa were kneeling on the floor, and the tambourine player had been joined by another musician, playing a long bamboo flute. Every now and again the bookseller would change the rhythm by banging his hand on his knee, or he would raise the pitch of the responses by chanting higher and higher. After a while he banged on the floor with the flat of his hand. Immediately everyone began to chant "Allah, Allah." A young man stood up in the middle of the circle. I was doing my best to join in and to watch at the same time, which made things difficult. The bookseller caught my eye, smiled, and gave me a wink as the man in the center of the circle bowed to him, a deep bow almost to the ground. He began to turn, slowly at first, his arms folded across his chest. Little by little the spin grew faster; as the young man unfolded his arms the rhythm increased and the drumming became more and more intense. I was wearing a heavy woolen jacket, and found myself running with sweat. I was kneeling in an awkward position, my legs were cramping. I would have loved to stop, but the men on either side

carried me forward and backward in the rhythm until I lost all sense of my body. All I could hear was the call of "Allah" reverberating through me; all I could see was a light spreading everywhere. The Dervish who was spinning was completely balanced, with his head tilted slightly back and to the left. His eyes were gleaming. Occasionally he would cry out. I felt that at any moment I might lose consciousness and there would be nothing left but the sound of the word and this intense light that continued to grow. But then, just at the peak of intensity, the Dervish stopped spinning quite suddenly. He did not seem to be giddy at all. He just came to a halt, crossed his arms over his chest, and bowed deeply. The drumming stopped, the zikr died down, and the men on either side of me were kissing my hands. The room vibrated with love and joy, as though each person were greeting the others after a long separation.

Following this, I was greeted by each person in the room, and as coffee was being served, a young man introduced himself to me. "My name is Farid," he said. "I speak English, and I will be happy to act as translator for you and our Sheikh." The room quickly fell silent as everyone began to listen to our conversation.

"Please give him my thanks," I began, "for allowing me to be here with all of you." The Sheikh accepted my gratitude solemnly, and it was not necessary for Farid to translate his reply. Everyone in the room smiled at me with great kindness.

I had some trouble in phrasing the question I most wanted to ask. "Please ask the Sheikh," I said finally, "whether he is the Sheikh I was sent to find in Istanbul. And if he is, why did he not tell me then." The question was translated, and the Sheikh responded with a roar of laughter. He leaned forward and spoke with Farid. "Our Sheikh says, 'Of course I am.' "

"Why did you not tell me then that I had accomplished my goal, and allow me to pay my respects to you?"

"There is a saying in the Koran, 'We will try them until we know.' I wanted to find out whether it was Allah's wish that we meet or not. I knew that if it was He would guide us to be together again, and so I was quite happy to wait."

"But I was told that the Sheikh worked in a tailor's shop, and yet you work in a bookshop. How is that?"

The Sheikh smiled again. "You must understand that I never heard of the man who sent you from England, and I have never worked in a tailor shop. His information was not quite correct, but then you found me anyway, and that is all that matters."

Each time a sentence was translated all the Dervishes leaned forward so as not to miss a word of the conversation. For the next hour or so the atmosphere in the room was electric. The Sheikh explained that he had never heard of Hamid, and denied any intuitive knowledge that we were going to meet. I asked him if he had come to Knoya at that time for any special reason, and he told me that he came quite frequently to see his friends and that was the only reason.

"Why were you walking toward the square this morning?" I persisted.

"To visit Shams–i Tabriz, the same reason as yourself," he replied. "Whenever I have the chance I always go to pay my respects, but that was the first time I have ever found the tomb closed."

I told him how I had gone there the day before and all that had transpired from that moment, trying to explain as simply as possible why I was searching, and the things that I had done during my life that had led me to this moment. "You are too serious," he said. "Why are you so serious? Do you think that He has not got a sense of humor? He must be laughing very much at this moment to see an Englishman here with us asking all these questions when He knew, at the beginning, that all this was going to happen.

"Now tell me, is this the first time that you have met the Dervishes?"

I explained that my original object had been to find out if the Dervishes had any knowledge of healing, since that was a subject that had absorbed me a great deal, but since then so many other things had happened that finally I was looking only to find my real self, to discover what use I could be in the world.

"Ah," he said. "Now if you had searched just to try to gather some information for yourself you would never have found us, and that is why your teacher kept you waiting for so long. No doubt he will have told you that knowledge is given and not acquired and that we do not welcome people who come to try to take knowledge. We will even lead them astray and send them on useless errands so that they will not find what they are looking for. Such things as healing are very interesting, but we must remember that the first thing of all is God, from Whom everything else follows. Dervishes are proud people, and, as you know, their meetings are illegal in this country. You have been allowed here only because of the sincerity of your motive."

I was still puzzled. How, if the Sheikh had not heard of Hamid, had Hamid heard of him? I asked about this as carefully as I could. The question sent the whole room into fits of laughter.

"But why do you laugh?" I asked plaintively.

"If you were not from the West," the Sheikh replied, "you would not have asked the question in the first place. The answer is easy for all of us here, but it is not possible for me to tell you. If I tried to explain, then I would have to explain with reason, and the answer has nothing to do with reason."

Although the young man who was translating for us occasionally had difficulty finding the correct English words, he seemed thoroughly familiar with concepts that I was finding so difficult.

I tried again, with a different question. "I still don't understand. How did Hamid know of you, and know that I would find you?"

The Sheikh was silent for a moment. Then he said, "I will tell you a story. If you can understand it, you will have the answer to your question.

"In the beginning of time there was the word, and the word was spoken by God, and the word was 'Be!' From that moment everything started to come into being. In that moment all creation that would ever be, simply was, and in that word was all that was necessary for everything we see to come about, and for us to see beyond this world into the real world. So in the beginning is everything. Yet what you see here and now is not the real world, and what I say to you, if you listen to the form of the words, is not real either. If, on the other hand, you listen to the sighing of the wind, you will hear the message of truth. If you send your message on the wind, then sooner or later someone will be attentive enough to pick it up. You cannot necessarily know who will hear; and yet, in Reality, there is only Him, and so it is He Himself who hears the message, and it is He Himself who sends it. Now listen to the sound of the wind."

The Sheikh put his finger to his lips and the room grew very still. "Listen," he repeated, "and you will hear the carrying sound of telepathy."

Gradually the room filled with sound—the sound that began all sounds. It was the sound *"Hu,"* and it was the sound behind the wind. It was everywhere. I was not searching anymore. The sound carried the search, and the message itself was the sound *"Hu."* The art of transmitting an idea from one person to another across space is just another subtle form of language, and all language comes from the first command of God when he brought the world into being. That is why the Dervishes had laughed at my question. It was not a matter of whether Hamid had heard of the Shaikh at all; that was not important. What was important was that we were together, all of us, and the mystery behind all of this was not the key that would unlock the door. The moment itself would unlock the door. Although I had asked a question about communication, what I had really asked was, "Why am I here, please," and so the answer could be given in the way that it was.

There seemed to be one more question to ask the Sheikh. It was a question that had been on my mind for a long time.

"What," I asked, "is a Dervish?"

He looked at me, and there was a long silence before he spoke again. "We speak in story form, as you know," he said, "and one of the reasons for this is that you can listen to a story over and over again, for each moment is different and will not repeat itself. Therefore the story will mean something different each time you study it. It depends on the mood you are in, the place you are looking at the story from, the time of day—many things, and so the story that I tell you will have no interpretation. You must listen to it, study it, and then, one day, you may understand."

The Sheikh continued, "Once there was a swarm of mosquitoes. The wind blew, and, since the window of the Sheikh's house was open, all the mosquitoes blew in with the wind. On the other side of the room was another open window, and the mosquitoes that had blown in one window were blown out the other—all except for one. That one landed on the Sheikh's wife's knee. The Sheikh looked, smiled, raised his hand, and killed it. The mosquito that died became the Dervish."

With that he stood up, and, saying a prayer over all of us, brought the meeting to a close. Beckoning to me and Farid, he led us out into the street.

"I have something to say to you," he began. "I am going to return to Istanbul tonight. If you like, you may come with me."

"That is very kind of you, but I promised to visit the three tombs, and I don't think I should leave until I have done so."

"The tombs have been closed to you twice," he said, "so perhaps it is not intended that you go to them just yet. There may be something that you must do before you will be quite ready for that moment. If you like, you and Farid and I can drive to Istanbul together. It is up to you."

The young man was having a hard time concealing his excitement, but I did not know what to do, for I was torn between a longing to go on talking with the Sheikh and the feeling that I should stay in Konya to carry out my instructions.

"I will leave from the square at seven o'clock this evening. If you are there, we can go together."

With that he took the translator's arm; they waved to me, and I was left alone.

nine

True Knowledge comes of three things—a tongue which repeats the name of God, a heart which is grateful, a patient body.

—Aflaki
The Whirling Ecstasy

Reason is the illusion of reality.
—Hazrat Inayat Kahn

And protect your heart from being inclined toward what you have renounced of people and desires and wishes and option and effort and from losing patience and harmony and pleasures with God at the time of the befalling of calamity.
—Abdul Qadir Gilani

I found it very difficult to make up my mind, because any form of logical reasoning seemed impossible. The thought of accompanying the Sheikh to Istanbul was very exciting, but there was still my promise. So much had happened in the past two weeks that instead of an easy flow of events, one into another, all order had disappeared. Without order it is almost impossible to make a conscious decision, but it was slowly dawning on me that we are almost incapable of making conscious decisions in this world anyway. We have the feeling that we can make some sort of decision between this and that or to take a journey here or there, yet there is another way of life that requires only that one abandon oneself to be carried to wherever we should be. The decision is made for us, in the moment that we sacrifice our own will to the greater Will.

I was only now coming to know what it meant to surrender as a living experience. Because I had left England and my own past behind, had taken the plunge into the unknown, I was now being given a chance for an understanding of how the real world unfolds itself into this relative world. In normal terms the events of the past weeks made no sense at all. The almost ceaseless traveling, the series of coincidences that could not be explained, the meetings with these strange people who seemed to be pieces of a jigsaw puzzle; all these things served to show my doubting mind a truth that could not be denied—there are laws governing our existence about which we have no understanding at all. Our lives are ruled by forces which, although invisible and intangible, have power greater than anything that can be seen or experienced in the physical world. Hamid had said that there was another language, the language of the heart; so there must be a way of understanding, with direct insight rather than with discursive reasoning. As I walked along the cold winter streets of Konya that day I felt the inevitability of all that I had experienced; if I could keep from interfering with the passage of events by using my own will or by trying to analyze everything, then I would be led to the greater knowledge for which I searched.

It was late in the afternoon when I returned to the hotel resolved to just let go, to relax and let events show me what I should do.

I lay down on my bed and stared at the ceiling, with the sound of the zikr running through my mind; the room seemed filled with the tremendous sense of dignity and presence of the Dervishes I had met. It was like nothing I had ever known, and I felt that if only every human being could know the intensity of love for God that these people felt, then a real change could come about, a new society could be built, based on love and knowledge rather than on fear, ambition, and greed. It was not a question of copying the Dervishes in their practices but rather of learning to live life passionately as they did and of bringing that understanding into each moment of our lives.

When I awoke it was dark. I had no recollection of falling asleep. Panic seized me. Half awake and trembling, I fumbled around for my watch. It was nine P.M. The meeting time had been seven P.M.!

Without stopping to think I pulled my clothes from the hangers, shoving them into the suitcase, feeling that it was vital that I get to Istanbul at once. My mind seemed set on this, and when I tried to consider whether I should stay another day in Konya there was not doubt at all but that I must get to Istanbul.

The man at the desk seemed surprised at my haste, and asked whether I had had dinner. "It is necessary that you eat, no?"

"No," I said, "I don't want food—I must get to the bus station right away. If there's no bus now, I will wait there until one comes."

I paid my hotel bill, caught a taxi, and fifteen minutes later I was at the bus station. Running to the ticket office, I inquired about a bus to Istanbul. "You want to go now?" asked the man. "Yes, of course, but when does the bus leave?" "Well, sir, the bus has already gone, just five minutes ago. But another bus is coming because there were too many people to go on the first one. So you can go on the second bus if you like."

In the rush of getting out of the hotel I had just allowed myself to get to where I had to be, and now here was a special bus, and there was a seat. Obviously the whole thing was intended, and it did not matter that I had not gone to the tombs. It was a great relief, and I sat back in the seat with a sense of ease that I had not felt for a long time. I was on my way back to Istanbul, and soon I would be with Hamid once again. I felt so happy that the long journey passed quickly. Even the discomfort of the bus seat did not bother me, and I slept most of the way.

We entered the outskirts of Istanbul just before dawn. The streets were filling with the traders who lined up to catch the early risers on their way to work. The stalls in the open markets were already doing good business, selling fruit of all kinds, fresh vegetables, and bread still hot from the ovens. The minarets resounded with the early morning call to prayer. This time my arrival in Istanbul was not threatening, but more like a homecoming. I felt happier than I had been since the journey started. Nothing seemed ugly to me; even the noise of the traffic and the jostling and pushing in the street appeared beautiful that morning. Despite my lack of sleep, and the events of the day before, I was not tired. The flow of energy that passed through me seemed to touch others as well, for people turned and smiled as we got off the bus at the terminal and one of the passengers offered me a bag of fruit. It was a good day, and had every promise of continuing that way.

I found a taxi without difficulty and gave the driver the address of Hamid's cousin, where he had said he would be staying. "You must cross the water by ferry," he had told me, "and then take a bus which will drop you right at the door." I tried to explain all this to the driver, but he spoke neither English nor French. He just smiled at me, baring huge yellow teeth with endless gold fillings, and drove at tremendous speed along the streets. I kept telling him that he should take me to the ferry so that I could cross over the Bosphorous, and then find the bus. Stupidly, I had not asked him what he was going to charge me. When he drove on board one of the ferries I realized that it was too late to turn back and that he was intending to drive me the whole way. What on earth was this trip going to cost, I wondered, but there was nothing to be done about it now; I just sat back and tried to stop worrying.

It was another three quarters of an hour before we pulled

up at the address I had given him. The bill was so enormous that I could not pay it all. I tried to explain that I would have to knock on the door of the house and try to borrow some money. The driver was looking very angry and his smile had become an ominous stare as he held onto my suitcase and pointed at my pocket. "Wait, wait," I said, "I won't be a moment," and pointed to the house. In the excitement of arriving in Istanbul I had forgotten that it was quite early in the morning and that people would perhaps still be sleeping. There was no answer to the doorbell, so I tried knocking on the curtained windows. Still no answer. What if nobody was home! By this time the driver was shouting and threatening me with the police and a small crowd had gathered around the car. "Friend, friend," I said, pointing at the house, but still there was no answer. Someone came out of the crowd and spoke to me in English. "The driver says that he has driven you right across Istanbul, and he wants you to pay him." "I know," I said, "but I have run out of money and my friend in there," pointing to the door once again, "will be able to help." "The driver says that if you do not pay him at once he will call the police." "Look, I have heard that," I tried to explain, "but first I must find my friend and then everything will be all right." The man from the crowd did not show any emotion; it was as though he had not heard me at all. "The driver says that he does not like the Americans." "But I am not American," I answered, "I am English." This was all being translated for the benefit of the crowd, which was growing larger. "The driver says that he does not like the English either. He likes the Germans." "I don't care a damn who he likes or does not like," I shouted at him. "Please tell him that it is all going to be fine and that he will get his money right away."

With that I banged on the door with such force that the windows shook. "Hamid, Hamid," I shouted. This time the door opened a little and a familiar face looked out. It was the girl.

Her disheveled hair, and the pain in her eyes, caught the

attention of the crowd. As she stepped out into the street, dressed in the same long white gown she had worn in Sidé, the talking and shouting ceased. The driver stopped his gesticulating but continued to hold tightly to my suitcase. The translator stood just behind me, his mouth hanging open. One by one, the crowd turned and moved silently away. "It's all right," I said to the driver, "just wait a moment."

I eased my way past the girl, who remained looking down the street, passing the ball of wool thoughtfully from hand to hand. "Hamid," I called out again.

He came out of a room on the left, pulling on a dressing gown over his pajamas. He did not look surprised, nor did he welcome me. The coldness of his greeting wiped away all that remained of the joy that I had experienced early that morning. I explained my predicament, and he went back into this room, returning in a moment to hand me two hundred lira. Then he went after the girl, who had walked out into the street. The crowd had dispersed, and the driver was now back in his car. Some children had come up and were playing around the girl, imitating her slow walk and silent movements. She seemed unaware, walking slowly up the street, her gown caught by the morning breeze. Hamid brought her back into the house and took her quietly upstairs. I traded the driver the two hundred lira for my suitcase, expecting and receiving no change. Then I followed them into the house.

The dining room, built high out over the Bosphorous, was flooded with light from the early morning sun. It was filled with wonderful antiques, French furniture and sculpture, eighteenth century paintings on the walls. Outside, the Bosphorous swirled its way past the French windows, a hive of activity that morning. Tiny fishing boats drifted with the tide, the fishermen holding long lines off the sterns. Children played in the back eddies by the wall in the next garden, launching paper boats and splashing in the shallows. The Bosphorous is about a mile wide at that point, and everywhere there were boats, big tankers flying Russian flags, small tramp steamers laden to the gunwales, barges piled high with coal, luxury cruise liners anchored out in the middle of the water, their passengers being unloaded into smaller craft. There were fishing boats, speedboats, tugs and row boats and ferries, moving so close to the front of the house that I could see the faces of of the people below decks looking out through the glass viewing panels. The view was so engrossing that I did not hear Hamid enter the room.

"Well?" he asked.

He had brushed his hair and changed his pajamas for a loose-fitting Turkish shirt over blue trousers. I started by apologizing and explaining how the taxi driver had taken me across on the ferry because it had been impossible to explain to him what I wanted. Hamid listened for a while, told me that I was an idiot, and then suggested breakfast. Of the girl he did not say a word. The atmosphere in the room reminded me of the time on the mountain when he had become so angry. While he was out of the room preparing breakfast I tried to center myself and not to react to the fear that was mounting inside me. Something was wrong, I knew. In the hotel in Konya I had felt quite sure that I was doing the right thing, but now everything was different. Perhaps I had made a mistake again and I would be asked to leave.

My mind was preoccupied with these thoughts, but nothing was said over the breakfast table. We ate bread and fruit and drank thick, sweet Turkish coffee. It was not until we had finished eating that Hamid spoke to me.

"Now you will please tell me all that has happened since last we met."

I tried to remember all that had transpired since I had left him in Sidé, looking back over the days and hours to fill in the details. He seemed to want to know everything, just where I had stayed, what food I had been eating, who I had met, and so on. I told him about the tombs being closed and of my meeting with the Sheikh. This seemed to interest him not at all. He gestured impatiently at my description of the zikr and returned to the subject of the tombs, cross-examining me again as to the times of my visits and the reasons that the tombs had been closed.

"And why did you not stay another night so that you could do what I told you to?" he asked. "Do you think that I sent you all the way to Konya for nothing? What about the Dervish you met at the amphitheater in Sidé? Do you think it was just coincidence that you met him and that he mentioned Mevlana to you? You are so thick—thick, and stupid, and you don't listen. You have forgotten the purpose for which you came to me. Once more you have wasted my time, and this is the last time. Will you please learn that you are not here to waste my time or anyone else's, and you are not here to go on your own trip, or to think you know anything at all. You are here to be introduced into the Way, as you yourself requested. So far you have been tested and mainly you have failed. You failed the test of courage up on the mountain, which was also a test of trust, and still you could not see. You keep looking at the form of this world, just as you insisted that a rock in the road had damaged the car. You say you trust me, but you deny that trust again and again. What sort of pupil are you, anyway? I should have sent you back to England and your antique business weeks ago. You simply will not listen. Can you not understand that all creation is and always will be in one moment of time? This means that what can be accomplished in a week depends entirely on our degree of trust and on getting rid of our own little wills for a greater and higher will—the Will of God."

"But Hamid—" I began.

"Don't interrupt me," he roared. "You have got me into all sorts of trouble because of your lack of trust, and now your lack of patience. If you had stayed one more day in Konya you might have been received. But now you are back here, having achieved nothing at all, and we will have to start all over again."

I tried to tell him why I had returned to Istanbul, but found that I didn't really have an explanation. "You see, the Sheikh said that I could travel to Istanbul with him, and he said that as the tombs had been closed twice, perhaps it was not the right time for me to visit them. So I thought that I could go back another time."

"You thought nothing! You did not do what you were asked to do, and you did not think at all. I have been watching you very carefully these past weeks and I see that you are still caught in the world of attraction. You want to come to know God, do you? You want to come into Being, to come to love?"

"Yes, Hamid, I do."

"Then you must understand that you cannot come to love through attraction. You could not see that you were caught by your craving for phenomenal or psychic experience, and therefore you went to the zikr and thought that it was all wonderful and that your journey had been fulfilled."

"But it *was* wonderful, Hamid. . . ."

"Wonderful it might have been, but that was not why you were sent to Konya. I keep telling you—you still have not got over the world of attraction. First you must come into the knowledge of yourself, and that cannot be discovered through attraction alone. Love without knowledge is only a little better than useless. First you must have knowledge, and then you are led, inevitably, to love. If you try to do it the other way around, there is a very real danger of reverting to an elemental state. Do you remember my warning to you about the condition of the world today? It is your responsibility to look after your world—and it is also your responsibility not to revert to a condition that is below your dignity. Do you understand what I mean?"

I found myself quite confused. It was true that I had been attracted to the zikr, and to the world of the Dervishes, but had Hamid not set me on this path himself, when he had sent me in search of the Sheikh in Istanbul? I asked him about this.

"Did you not tell me," he answered, "that the Sheikh, or whoever he is, said that he did not know me?"

"Yes," I replied.

"Then is your question not answered? I sent you to the

Sheikh to see whether or not you would find him. I knew that if you were to find him, then you were still bound to the world of attraction and would be caught in the glamour of it all. If you did not find him, then you would be free of that and could go on. The trouble is that you do not yet turn straight to God. You are still using your own will, and that is where the trouble lies. If you were to turn, then you would know that you will be given exactly what you need to do His will. Certainly the zikr was wonderful, a great experience for you. But what was the original intention of your journey to Konya? You were to go and pay your respects to the three saints. What actually happened was this: when you experienced the zikr with the group of Dervishes you immediately got caught in your own will, your own craving for experience. Surely that is a trap! Instead of staying on in Konya until the tombs were open to you, you became caught by the idea of going to Istanbul with the Sheikh so that perhaps you would be allowed to do the zikr with him again. Is this not so?"

"But if I have been given what I need, why are you so angry, Hamid?"

"Ah," he said, wagging his index finger under my nose, "although in Essence everything is perfect, down here in this world it is another matter. You could easily have passed the test if you had been sensible. As it is you have wasted time, and waste, as I am always telling you, is the only real sin. Everything follows from that.

"Now you must go away and learn a little about patience. I'm afraid that you can't stay in this house anyway. My cousin comes back from her trip today, and the girl is here, as you know. You will just have to go to a pension nearby and wait there."

"But, Hamid," I protested, "I can't afford to stay in a pension. I don't have very much money left."

"Then send for more," he said. "You have money in England, or at least you have furniture or something. Sell it and pay your way. Everyone on this path must be self-supporting.

Do you expect me to support you? Now this is the address of the pension." He handed me a piece of paper. "It is possible to walk there, but with your suitcase perhaps it would be better to take the bus. Cable for your money, and go and wait in the pension until I send for you."

"How much money should I send for? How long will I be at the pension?"

"I haven't the slightest idea," he replied. "I am not the judge, and it depends on many things. Now please go. I have work to do."

Living in that pension on the Bosphorous with nothing to do, nowhere to go, not even books to read, I began to understand how totally impotent we are in this world until there is real change in us. Day after day I would get up early, do the various practices that Hamid had taught me over the past year, and do some physical exercises to try to keep myself in shape. The pension, like the other house, was built right on the water's edge, but my room was a little hut in the back, overlooking the stone courtyard where a huge Alsatian dog was chained to the wall. He was never freed, but each time someone knocked at the gate he would run the full length of his chain, barking and growling, only to be brought up just short of the person trying to come in. Then the owner would come down, pull the dog back, and the guest could enter. This scene was enacted many times each day, and although the chain did not quite reach to the door of my room I had to edge my way along one side of the patio, since the dog behaved with me in the same way that he behaved to those entering from the street.

After the practices in the morning I would go to the main house and have breakfast. My money arrived from England after about a week; somehow the fact that I now had enough money for an almost indefinite period didn't lift my spirits. There was absolutely nothing to do, and no one in the pension spoke either English or French. Most of the residents went off to work early in the morning and returned just in time for the evening meal, which was served on the enclosed veranda. Dinner time was the best time of day, for we would sit out and watch the boats and, when the weather was fine, see the sun go down. Most of the time it rained, though, and a cold wind blew in through the cracks in the windows. Day after day I sat there, eating the meals that were put in front of me with little interest in the food. Sometimes I would sleep late out of sheer endless boredom. I could see that this was a test—but the point of the test had been forgotten, and if it had not been for the fear of what would happen I would have chucked the whole thing then and there and gone back to England. Hamid was only a few minutes down the road, but the telephone never rang for me. There were no letters, no messages. Absolutely nothing.

In time, if you have no work to do, and nowhere to go, and no one to talk to, there comes a moment when you realize that indeed you are completely useless. You might have believed that you had some mission, or some inner voice to tell you that you were doing the right thing, or some preconceived notion of what it means to try to help your fellow men. But when you are left alone, under orders to simply wait for an indefinite period, you begin to realize just how little you actually know.

For the first few days my mind raced round and round, as I tried to go back over the events that had brought me to this point. For hours I would dwell on one particular aspect of the journey, trying to see if I could make sense out of it. I would try to figure out if I really did trust Hamid, or whether I was fooling myself. At times I thought that I actually hated him. He was such an enigma, and although he had told me that I must surrender my will to God's will, it seemed that I had sacrificed my own free will to *him*, not to God. Now I was trapped, with no will of my own. I was doing what I had been told, but now the question rose in my mind, Did Hamid really know what he was doing? Perhaps, I thought, he is leading me astray. I had imagined that on this path I would be able to sort out some of my own problems and learn to live more easily. Quite the reverse had happened. If I had had any peace of mind before coming to Turkey, I certainly had none now. Here I was, stuck in the middle of Istanbul, not knowing what would happen or whether anything that I had been through was of any benefit at all. I did not know how long I was being asked to stay in the pension; it could be for months—perhaps even years! And this prospect led me to hours and days of despair again. I even began to fantasize about how I would kill myself, as I felt more and more useless. Then I got the flu.

For a week I was too ill to get out of bed. The owner of the pension brought me soup and fruit, but I was almost too weak to raise my head, and I could scarcely swallow. Since I did not get any better and was running a high fever, he insisted on bringing in a doctor who gave me penicillin shots, charged me exorbitantly, and returned every day to repeat the performance. I got weaker and weaker, so that when the fever eventually did go down I could scarcely walk across the yard. The owner was not very sympathetic—he was worried about the responsibility of having me there, and he was quite suspicious of me anyway because all I ever did was to sit about or sleep all day.

After another week I began to feel a bit stronger and the weather had grown delightfully springlike. There had been no word from Hamid, and by now I was convinced that I had failed whatever test I had been given. I was weak, I had lost weight, I had ceased to care one way or the other whether I was on the spiritual path or off it, and I was no longer really interested in finding out the "Truth"—whatever that might be. I wanted to just get the hell out of that place as soon as I was strong enough and go back to England to try to take up my life where I had left it. Life had become pointless, the whole journey had become a nightmare rather than an adventure, and although I kidded myself that I had the courage to call Hamid I knew that really I was too scared to pick up the phone.

Finally, one day when the sun was really warm, I decided

to go for a trip up the Bosphorous. To hell with Hamid and all his practices—after all, the trip and the fresh air would do me good. I was still weak and had a nasty cough, so I decided that a trip to the Black Sea would be just what I needed. At last I gathered up a little more courage and telephoned Hamid to tell him what I planned to do.

He did not react to my call or to the news of my illness. "It's such a nice day, Hamid," I said, "that I thought I would take a little trip up the Bosphorous to get some fresh air."

"What a good idea," he replied. "I do hope you have a nice day."

It was all right! For the first time in my several weeks at the pension I felt happy and elated. I walked down to the quay where the boats came in, took the first one heading up the Bosphorous, and spent a perfect day, stopping off at little towns along the way, taking the ferry from one to another.

I did not return to the pension until after dark. I had been back scarcely ten minutes when the owner knocked on my door to let me know that I had a telephone call.

It was Hamid. His voice was cold and distant on the other end. "While you were away someone came to see you. It was a pity that the person could not wait and so has gone away again." I heard the click of the telephone on the other end.

My room was lonelier than ever before. All my good spirits had been replaced by the old despair. What could it mean that someone had come to see me? I did not know anyone in Istanbul except for the Sheikh, and surely it would not have been him. Hamid had sounded as though I had failed a test—yet instead of yelling at me or ordering me to go home he had just left me dangling once more. That night I ordered wine to be brought to my room. I drank the whole bottle, and when I finally fell asleep it was with the resolution to leave for England the next morning.

By morning my mood was somewhat better, and I decided to make one last attempt to fulfill whatever it was that I had been sent to the pension to achieve. The test had to do with patience, I was sure, but I also felt that there was more to it than that.

But when another week had dragged past in tedium I decided to go up the Bosphorous for a second time. Again I called Hamid, and again he said that he thought the trip a fine idea, as I was still not quite recovered from the flu. Again I thought that things would be all right. And again when I returned that night Hamid telephoned me. "While you were away, they came," he said.

The next morning I packed my bags, telephoned the airport, and booked a flight to England for the following day. I wished that I didn't have to see Hamid again, even to say good-bye, but I knew that I must.

When I knocked at Hamid's door it was opened by an older woman who turned out to be his cousin. "Come in," she said, "we've been expecting you. Lunch will be ready soon. You will stay?" She took me into the living room, gave me a glass of sherry, and in a little while Hamid came in. "There you are," he said, embracing me warmly. "Goodness, but you are thin. But then this flu does take so much out of one. And I suppose the doctor will have given you penicillin, which only makes things worse. Still, you are quite recovered now?"

Lunch was brought in and we dined as though everything were perfectly normal. No mention was made of the pension; Hamid and his cousin talked about the world crises, and Turkish and Greek politics, and the sort of chit-chat that one might expect at a casual luncheon. When the coffee was brought, however, Hamid's cousin turned to me and said, "So, I am told that you want to be a pupil of the Way. Why would this be, that an Englishman and not even a Moslem would want to follow the Way? My cousin has been trying to explain, but it makes no sense to me at all. My own Sheikh always says that there is little chance for people like you since you will never give anything up. It is all too comfortable for you in the West. Is this not so?"

The last thing I wanted to do was to go into the journey and my reasons for it all over again, but the more I insisted that I was going to leave and go back to England, the more she insisted that I should explain. I had not even had the opportunity to tell Hamid of my decision. He sat across the table from me, listening impassively to my rationalizations. Finally he broke into the conversation and spoke rapidly to her in Turkish. Then, turning to me, he said, "You can go if you want, but I was going to arrange for you to see a very important man tomorrow. That is, if you wish. You have free choice, but it could be to your advantage."

"But I thought there was no more point in going on. I thought that because 'they'—whoever 'they' are—came and went while I was out that I had failed whatever the test was."

"Now you are using your own will again!" Hamid said irritably. "I tell you, you are not the judge. How do you know that you have failed the test when you do not even know what the test was? If you knew patience, you would understand. Can't you see that nothing can happen until the time is right? Now it is the right time to visit someone I have been wanting you to meet. You do not know whether you passed the test, and what is more you will not know until you find out whether this person will receive you or not. If you are received then it is all right. If not, then not. But you have free choice. Go back to England if you like. I personally do not care one way or the other."

With that he left the table and the room. Damn it! What was all this about? I had had enough of it—and now I was being offered more. In my frustration I went out of the room to try to find Hamid. He was sitting in the front room talking to his cousin. "All right," I said, "I will cancel my plane flight. But I do not understand."

"Good," he said, "then you can stay here for the night."

"You mean the girl has gone and there is room?"

"No, she is still here."

"But I thought you said there wasn't room for me."

"Did I?" he replied, smiling.

The next day Hamid, his cousin, and I took a car to visit the man that Hamid had mentioned. All I had been told of this man was that he was old and that he had no teeth. He was, however, very partial to soft-centered chocolates, so we stopped on the way to buy a box of very special chocolates that were made at the back of a small shop.

The only instructions I had been given were that I was to wear my best clothes, and that I was going to see someone who was very important in this journey. "You must be aware of everything that goes on," Hamid had said, "even if you do not understand what is being said. Just pay heed, and show proper respect. That is the important thing for today."

We drove in silence to the other side of Istanbul, to a residential part of the city, stopping outside a house set back from the road a little way. When Hamid knocked, the door was immediately opened by a woman who beckoned us into a large room, newly furnished and very modern in appearance. At one end of the room was a sofa, with a low table in front of it. The woman put the chocolates on the table and motioned us to be seated. The chair I was given was exactly opposite the center of the sofa. Soon several members of the family and some other guests entered. After the introductions, silence fell.

Soon the door opened and an old man came in. He was tall and thin, and his sparse hair was almost white. He was very frail, but the first thing you noticed were his eyes. They were dark and deep-set, and his gaze was compelling and direct. Stopping for a moment at the threshhold he looked round the room, greeting each person silently with those extraordinary eyes, holding each of us for a moment and then moving on to the next person. His wife took his arm and helped him across the room to the sofa, where he sat down opposite me. He said nothing, but leaned back and breathed deeply for a few moments. His wife, who sat on a chair to his right, bent forward, opened the box of chocolates, and handed them to him. He smiled, obviously pleased, but insisted that each of us take one before he would help himself. I was fascinated by the way he chewed on the chocolate with his gums, for it was true that he had no teeth.

After what seemed a very long time he turned to Hamid and asked him a question. A two-way conversation followed, with frequent references to names that I had heard before, and particularly to Mevlana Jelalu'ddin Rumi and to Konya. Finally the old man leaned back on the sofa and closed his eyes. He seemed to be resting; the silence was complete, and everyone in the room had closed his eyes. I did the same, trying to be open to whatever was going on. After a few minutes I felt someone nudging me. It was the wife of the old man. Smiling at me, she pointed to the sofa. He was getting slowly to his feet, supported on either side by a member of his family. When he had got his balance he began reciting something in Turkish, his eyes closed, his right hand reaching out in front of him. I felt a tremendous surge of emotion spread through me. It was like receiving a blessing. Then he opened his eyes and leaned foreward. Holding his hands above my head, he blew. "Hu," he breathed. Then, taking both my hands, he looked at me deeply, and as he did so he spoke again in Turkish. Two minutes later he had gone, helped out of the room by his wife, turning back once more to raise his hand to us all and to blow into the room.

Hamid leaned over to me. "It is all right," he said, "he has accepted you. He has said that you are to go to Konya immediately."

"But—I've already been to Konya."

"And you are to go back," he said. "You are to go to the tomb of Mevlana; having first prepared yourself by paying your respects to Shams–i Tabriz, you are to sit there for three days and three nights, to see if you will be received this time."

"What else did he say to me?" I asked. "I felt a blessing."

"Ah," Hamid replied, "it was a prayer for you, but I am afraid that I cannot tell you what it was. By the way, the person who came to see you while you were in the pension was a vegetable seller from the market. She came to our door

and said, 'I heard you have a friend staying with you who is very fond of vegetables. I have brought some for him.' So you see, if you had not gone out on the Bosphorous you would have learned something. Remember, there is only One Absolute Being, and He manifests Himself in different forms. I did not know the vegetable seller, but her arrival brought a message which told me something, and that is why I brought you here today."

With that we left, after bidding good-bye to the family. I did not ask who the old man was. It seemed superfluous, for I knew that something profound had happened, and there was really nothing to say. We drove back to the house in silence, and later that day I boarded the bus to Konya once again.

ten

As waves upon my head the circling curl,
So in the sacred dance weave ye and whirl.
Dance then, O heart, a whirling circle be.
Burn in this flame—is not the candle He?
—Mevlana Jelalu'ddin Rumi

Let Thy word, God, become my life's expression.
—Hazrat Inayat Kahn

The owner of the hotel welcomed me back as though I was a guest in his home, carrying my bags to the same room in which I had slept those weeks before. This time he insisted that I eat something, and brought up a tray of halva and honey cakes and Turkish coffee. He did not seem surprised to see me again, and was too well-mannered to ask me what I was doing. I knew that he was eager to know what an Englishman was doing back in Konya during the cold winter season, but there was no way that I could possibly explain even to myself how I came to be there once again.

That evening as I sat in my room after saying good night to the hotel keeper, my mind was preoccupied with my mission—to sit for three days and three nights outside the tomb of Mevlana Jelalu'ddin Rumi.

From my reading I knew that Konya had been the center of a great spiritual culture seven hundred years earlier, during the time of Rumi. Many of the great Sufi masters had congregated in that city, and all the major religions of the world had come into Asia Minor as though to a prearranged meeting of the ways, a knitting together of the inner truths that underlie the outer forms of religion. During that time Buddhism had been brought from China, and of course Konya had already been a great center for Judaism and Christianity as well as for Islam.

I had read that Rumi had been born in Persia in 1207 A.D., had settled in Konya, where he was reputed to have had ten thousand followers, and had died in 1273. Rumi's name is linked with that of Shams–i Tabriz, the "Sun of Tabriz." There are many stories of the first encounter of these two extraordinary men. One such story relates that, at their first meeting, Shams–i Tabriz seized the manuscripts of the books that were Rumi's life work until that point, and flung them down a well, saying, "Do you want them back? I promise they will be dry." At that moment of decision Rumi recognized Shams as his spiritual guide, and forsook the manuscripts that represented his past life. Leaving his family and his disciples, Rumi followed Shams into isolation for two and a half years. Rumi's disciples became jealous of Shams, and it is said that they finally killed him, although his body was never recovered. But by that time his job had been done; and for seven hundred years the influence of Rumi spread throughout the world, through his mystical writings and his poetry and through the order of Mevlevi Dervishes founded on his teachings.

This was really all I knew of him, and yet I could still not fully trust that the presence of this great Sufi Master might still exist so many hundreds of years after his death. Admittedly I had already had one experience of what it was like to be open to the living presence of someone who had died a long time before, but now I was remembering what Hamid had told me in England when he handed me the postcard, "One day, God willing, you will visit this place; if you do then you will know that your real journey has begun."

The next morning, having performed the ritual washing with extra care, I walked down the street toward the tomb of Shams-i Tabriz. This time the gates were unlocked. The square outside the building was empty. The wind blew scraps of paper around the trees, and a fine drizzle of cold rain made the pavements shine. Just outside the door stood a shoe rack, with three or four pairs of shoes arranged neatly on the shelves. I removed my shoes and stepped into the room. By the dim light of the oil lamps burning at the other end, I could just make out the silhouettes of a group of people praying.

Yet none of these details mattered, for as soon as I crossed the threshhold there was no avoiding the incredible presence that filled the room. It was like entering another dimension, where the power of love is so enormous that it seems to shatter all preconceived ideas, wipe clean the past, burst inside to unlock a door to the heart. I remember trying to pray; yet there was no need to say or do anything. It was only necessary to open myself, to allow this presence of love to enter. I do not know how long I stood there, nor do I have any recollection of leaving the place and starting on the walk to Rumi's tomb for my long vigil. One moment I was in the tomb of Shams–i Tabriz and the next I was in the courtyard of Rumi's tomb, sitting on a bench by the fountain, my fur coat pulled up tightly around my face for protection from the wind. I had gone through the outer gate, and crossed the courtyard to find the door to the tomb and the museum open. I had entered, seen the magnificence of the building and the tomb itself, familiar to me from the picture on the postcard that Hamid had given me in England, and then walked back into the courtyard, planning to begin my long vigil.

I had been sitting on the bench only a short time when I felt a tap on my right shoulder. Opening my eyes required a tremendous effort, and for a moment I could not focus them. When I did, I saw a man in uniform with a peaked cap bending over me and looking quite stern. "*Yok,*" he said. "*Yok* what?" I replied, not sure what was going on. "*Yok,*" he repeated firmly, standing up straight and pointing to the gate. I started to protest, but he cut me short, beckoning to another man in uniform. This time there was no doubt, for the other man spoke English. "I am most sorry, sir, but to sit at tombs is forbidden. So you go to visit Mevlana, and then we show you the museum, yes?"

"But you see," I tried to explain, "I have been asked to sit here. I mean I have been told to sit here for three days and three nights."

"Not possible. Please, you go now."

A crowd had collected and there was the usual heated discussion in Turkish. The first uniformed guide had turned his back on me and was telling them the story, and the second one was standing threateningly over me pointing to the gate. I had come several thousand miles from England, had traveled round Turkey, was apparently nearing the end of my journey, and had received special instructions from someone who was obviously important in Istanbul that I was to sit at the tomb for three days and three nights. I decided to hang on and not to move. The worst they could do would be to call the police, and by this time even the arrival of the whole police force did not seem important. I closed my eyes once more, breathed deeply, and tried to pretend that there was no one there.

For a few minutes this seemed to work but then I felt another tap on my shoulder, this time much harder, and then someone shaking my shoulder. I continued my meditation, trying to shrug him off. But then I heard another voice, so kind and gentle that I opened my eyes to see an old man with a gray beard and a blue pin-stripe suit, standing there and smiling at me.

The old man took both my hands in his, kissed them, and raised them to his forehead in greeting. Then he beckoned to someone at the back of the crowd. It was Farid, the young man who had acted as translator for my conversation with the Sheikh on my previous trip to Konya. We greeted each other warmly. I was so astonished to see him, and I had so many questions for him, that I could hardly speak at all.

The old man was explaining something to me in Turkish.

Farid listened for a moment, and then turned to me. "Dede says that he knew that you were coming. He says that you are to go with him to his house, where he has prepared a room for you. You are to come now, please, and I will come also to translate for you."

"But . . ." I started to protest. I was interrupted by a renewed flood of Turkish.

"Dede says that he knows that you have been given certain instructions, but he says that it does not matter anymore, and it is true that you are not allowed to sit here. Also the tomb closes in half an hour."

The old man was beaming at me as though I were a lifelong friend. "Please ask him," I said to Farid, "does he know the man in Istanbul who sent me here?" My question was translated to the old man, who burst into laughter, causing the crowd to laugh with him.

"He says of course he does—otherwise how would he know that you were coming?"

"But if they knew each other, why did the other man in Istanbul not know that it would not be possible for me to sit here to pay respects to Mevlana?"

"Dede says that he did know that it was not possible for you to sit here, but that what was important was the intention, not the sitting."

All this was being translated for the benefit of the crowd, which was fascinated with what was going on. Even the guides were beaming happily. Whenever the word Mevlana was spoken there was a moment of silence. I had become the center of attention and everyone wanted to talk to me. Farid turned from one person to another, explaining the situation as best he could. Finally, as the gates were closing, the crowd moved slowly away. The three of us left the tomb. Farid flagged down a taxi, and we drove away through the back streets of Konya.

The time that I spent with Dede (Dede means "Grandfather" or "old one") was a respite from the struggle, pain, and tension of the previous weeks. Dede's kindness, his trust, and acceptance of me as a friend, were always evident. It seemed that from the instant I entered the tomb of Mevlana it seemed that I had entered into calm waters after a storm that had lasted all my life.

Dede put no pressure on me, and seemed to want only to provide me the best possible opportunity for rest. His wife cooked simple meals in the evenings, and Farid was always on hand if needed. Most of our time, though, was passed in silence. We would get up early in the morning, go outside to

the water tap in the little yard, and perform the ritual washing. Then, at the call from the muezzin, Dede would perform his morning prayers. Later, after breakfast, the three of us would go together to the museum at the tomb of Mevlana. Pausing for a moment by the threshhold, Dede would cross his arms over his chest and bow before stepping inside. Farid explained to me that it was the tradition never to tread on the threshhold of any door, but rather to pause outside for a moment to leave your problems and tensions and negative emotions in the street, rather than bringing them into the house in which you are a guest. In one of the rooms, Dede would always bow to the lines of script that decorated the walls. One of these lines, Farid informed me, said, "Indeed God is Beautiful and loves the beautiful;" and another, "The sole purpose of Love is Beauty."

When we had proceeded around the different rooms of the museum, pausing at certain points, we would go out into the courtyard and he would speak about the life and teachings of Rumi.

Dede told me that the Way involves no form, although it may appear that certain rituals are followed. Farid explained, "Ours is a religion of love, and yet it is not religion in the way that you understand religion. We do not do our practices in order to come to realize God, but rather we accept the Unity of God first and then everything follows from that."

During that period, it seemed wrong for me to question Dede. After giving a discourse, or telling a story, he would smile and leave it to me to work out the inner meaning of his words. Once he told me that there were four levels of understanding and that it was up to me to listen with the greatest possible awareness so that I would not take things literally. "Dede says that most people understand only on the most obvious levels. They read the Koran or the sacred books and do not see that everything that has been written down has other, deeper meanings than what appears on the surface. You might read in the Koran about a battle and think that the story is only about a battle, but the battle was not just an historical event. It is now. If you see it in this way, then you can understand at the second level—allegorically. Dede says that if you listen to the stories that he tells, and know that they are actually illustrations of something else, then you may touch on their meaning and not just on their outward form, which is for those people who do not want to hear the truth, or else are not yet ready to accept all that the truth entails. Dede says that there are two further levels on which you can understand, the metaphysical and the mystical levels. Sometimes when he tells a story, however simple it is, he is telling it not only as an allegory but also to illustrate one of the great laws of the universe. Mevlana always spoke in this way and Dede wants you to study all of his works. He says that the deepest level of understanding is mystical. That is when it is not the words that count, not the allegory, nor even the laws of the universe, but when your heart is so deeply touched that the Truth which is within is experienced directly, in a state that is even beyond knowledge or conviction. Sometimes you will see Dervishes cry, because the beauty of God is almost too much to bear when you become completely absorbed in it."

Dede would sit in the courtyard outside the museum and speak of these things, nudging Farid to make sure that he understood the concepts he was translating. Then while the story or the discourse was spoken in English Dede would beam at me, watching every slightest move or reaction that I made. If I heard at the correct depth of understanding he would know it, and put his right hand over his heart and give a little bow.

These were wonderful days. Slowly the chaos that I had been experiencing re-formed itself into a new sense of order. Something was growing in me, and I began to see that it was the real "I" beginning to manifest after the stripping away of the veils. Dede told me of the training of the Mevlevi Dervishes, a course lasting 1,001 days, during which time they study philosophy, the humanities, the works of Mevlana, and the turn of the Dervishes. I resolved that if I ever had the chance I would return to Konya one day to study and to return to these people the love that I felt from them.

Sometimes in the evenings friends of Dede would come around and there would be story-telling and discussions late into the night. Only once did I meet with anything less than full acceptance. One of the guests who had come to the house kept looking over his shoulder at me, and talking in a low voice to Dede and Farid. I watched Dede getting very angry.

He was patient for a long time, trying to explain something to the man. I gathered that it was the usual question of whether or not I had embraced Islam. Finally Dede slammed his fist down on the brass coffee table in front of him, scattering the little cups, and shouted at the man. Farid turned to me and said, "The man asks whether you are an orthodox Moslem. Dede tells him that you believe in God and is that not enough?"

Since my first visit to Konya I had been fascinated by the "turn" of the Dervishes. In the hall outside Dede's room hung many old, framed photographs of Dervishes spinning in their tall hats and flowing white robes, their heads tilted slightly to one side. Dede had shown me pictures of his son turning at the great celebration held in December of each year to honor the coming into Union of Mevlana, their teacher and guide for seven hundred years.

I felt sure that there must be a reason behind this form of worship. Dede used to say that the cause of the tree is the fruit and not the roots, since the tree was planted for the fruit and not for the roots. "And the cause of the universe being brought into existence in love is man," he said. "That is, man who has come to love God perfectly. He is called Perfected Man, for there is really nothing left of him; there is only the eternal presence of God." If this was so, then when the Dervish was turning, spinning round and round in the state of ecstasy that I had witnessed, there must be something much deeper than just the experience; and this hidden secret was what I wanted to discover.

One day we were sitting in Dede's room, drinking coffee, when he turned to me and said something in Turkish. "Dede says that you should learn the turn," Farid informed me. Then the old man waved his hands and pointed to the floor, signifying that I was to stand in the middle of the room. Rather embarrassed, I stood up, and Dede moved his hand round and round in an anti-clockwise direction with the index finger pointing outward to show which way the turn went. "Dede says that you should start to turn very slowly. He says that you should cross your arms over your chest as you do when you enter the museum. Do you understand?" As I had been taught, I crossed my arms, placing my right hand on my left shoulder and my left hand on my right shoulder. "Dede says that you should practice with your arms as they are now. Please try it."

With as much dignity as possible I turned round to my left. I had made only two or three turns when I became so giddy that I had to stop. This caused them both tremendous amusement, and Dede began to speak again. "You see," Farid translated, "it is important that you make yourself a center right in the middle of your chest, here. . . ." He pointed to my chest. "If you do not make the center there you will get sick and you will fall over. Only if you are in the right place can you turn in the correct way. The left foot must never leave the floor. In the old days when you were taught the turn, a big nail would be driven into the floor between your big toe and the next one and you would have to turn round the nail so that your foot never left the ground. That is because the work of a real Dervish is here, on this earth. The Koran tells us, 'Stand proud in this world but bow in the next.' You must be the balance between this world and the world to come. Now please try again."

Putting all my concentration on the point in the center of my chest I closed my eyes and tried to turn around, with my left foot firmly anchored to the floor.

"No, your eyes open, please."

I started again, and found that it was much easier with my eyes open.

"Now you must learn to pick up the right foot so that it comes up behind the left leg and then you put it down the other side of the leg. It is as though your body turns to where you put your foot. But it is difficult, and will take you much time to learn."

This time, as I concentrated on the placement of my right foot, I lost my balance, and forgot completely about centering in the heart. I became giddy, thought I was going to be sick, and sat down abruptly. Dede was enjoying himself thoroughly, rolling about with laughter. Then he spoke with Farid for a few moments.

"Dede says that he will turn for you, but he is an old man and so his arms do not go up properly anymore. He says that if you want to learn, his son will teach you, but that it would take at least six weeks of hard work. Then, perhaps, you would go to England and teach them how to turn?"

The old man got slowly to his feet. He walked across to a cupboard at the side of the room, leaned inside, and drew out a black robe and a tall hat of beige felt. Handing the hat to Farid, he took the robe, spread it in front of him, and kissed it before putting it on. Farid handed him the hat and he walked slowly, in silence, to the center of the room. Then he crossed his arms, bowed low, and began very slowly to revolve. It was an effortless, easy-flowing motion that reminded me of a boat turning in the current of a river moving to the sea. Then, little by little, the spin grew faster until there came a moment when he uncurled his arms so that the right hand was raised, palm up, and the left pointed to the ground. It was incredibly beautiful, like the unfolding of a perfect flower. His left foot never left the floor, and although his arms were not raised as high as those of the young Dervish I had seen the last time I had been in Konya, there was such a gentle dignity to his movement that both Farid and I were touched. Dede's head was tilted a little to the left, his eyes open, and yet his gaze was nowhere in space. He was bowing in another world, but his body was turning in this. When he stopped he bowed once more and then, taking off his robe and kissing it once again, he handed the hat and robe to Farid and sat down quietly.

"Now," he said, "I will tell you a little more about the turn."

During the translation that followed, Dede interrupted frequently so that the point was made quite clear, and he would ask for my comments to be repeated back to him.

"It is like this," he said. "When you turn you do not turn for yourself but for God. We turn around in the way we do so that the Light of God may descend upon the earth. As you act as a channel in the turn, the light comes through the right hand, and the left hand brings it into this world. It is what you in the West call 'alchemy,' for if you concentrate correctly in your prayer to God then you make the necessary sacrifice of yourself. In this way light, which contains within itself perfect order, is able to come through onto the earth. We turn for God and for the world, and it is the most beautiful thing you can imagine.

"If you are quiet and in a state of prayer when you turn, offering everything of yourself to God, then, when your body is spinning, there is a completely still point in the center. In the knowledge that there is only Him, you can experience the universe turning around that center. When you turn, all the stars, and the planets, and the endless universes turn around that still point. The heavens respond; and all the invisible kingdoms join in the dance. Jesus said, 'Unless you dance you know not what cometh to pass.' That is why we turn. But the world does not understand. They think we turn in order to go into some sort of trance. It is true that sometimes we do go into that state you call ecstasy, but that is only when we know and experience at the same time. We do not turn for ourselves."

After that I practiced turning every day in the tiny room where we talked, and gradually I came to understand what Dede had told me about the turn. Dede's son was away and so it was not the proper time to practice all he had taught me. Rather it was time just to be, to let life unfold in a gentle way. One day slipped into another naturally, as slowly, it seemed, as the turn of the seasons. Little by little the shock of the past weeks was fading and the confusion I had felt, almost like a wound, was beginning to heal. I would have liked to stay there for a long time, just sitting and learning with this old man, but slowly I began to feel that in staying there I was denying something. Sooner or later I must return to Hamid, who had told me, just before I left Istanbul, that he would wait for me back in Sidé. It was becoming increasingly clear that this stage of the journey was nearly over. I was frightened about returning to Sidé, where I had experienced so much pain; the contrast in being with Dede and the easy daily routine of his household made my memories of Sidé seem raw and painful by comparison.

One morning when I awoke at dawn I found that my decision had been made. After the morning prayers and breakfast, I asked Dede if I might speak with him. Farid had gone away for a few days, but I felt that it was important that I ask Dede's permission to leave. He had grown so fond of me that I felt I was almost a member of his family, and my respect for him was so great that I did not want to do anything that might offend him.

I explained, in a mixture of sign language and the few words of Turkish I had picked up, that I felt that the time was right for me to go back to Sidé to be with Hamid. At first he did not understand, and then he realized that we needed a translator. Signaling that I was to remain in the house, he put on his coat and hat and set off down the street.

After a few minutes he returned with a man in his forties who spoke fluent English. After coffee and the usual exchanges I asked him to ask Dede if he would give me permission to return to Hamid.

Dede listened carefully to my words, and then to the translation. Then, taking both my hands as he had done that first day, he kissed them and raised them to his forehead. "Go with God, and with the blessing of Mevlana, and know that your home is here always." His eyes were filled with tears. For a little while we sat in silence, then he spoke again to the translator.

"Dede says he is sorry that you are going, but he knows that one day you will return. He says that it is your duty to go back to your teacher whom he does not know but who must be one of those who are seldom seen. He asks that you take his salaams to Hamid, and his thanks for sending you to Konya."

"But it was not he who sent me here," I interrupted. "It was the old man in Istanbul."

"Yes, but it was Hamid who took you to the old man whom Dede knows, and so it is to Hamid that thanks are due.

"Dede also says that you are never to forget that there is only One Being, only Allah; and so, in reality, all our thanks are to Him. He says that he wishes to give you something. Will you accept it?"

I did not know what to say. Sometimes it is very difficult to receive, and I was afraid that Dede was going to give me something that he owned, some precious possession. But I must accept, and I said that I would be greatly honored.

"Dede says that he wishes to give you a very humble gift and a message to go with it. He says that the one without the other is no good.

Leaning forward in his chair, the old man picked up an engraved brass box from the table and opened it carefully. He took out a beautifully shaped silver bottle with a sprinkler at the top, typical of the rose-water containers found throughout the Middle East. But this one was especially exquisite and he handed it to me with both hands, without taking his eyes from my face.

"Dede says that this is for rose water, the essence of the rose. He says that he feels you will understand, and he hopes that you will be able to give the rose water to your friends. His message to you is this: If you go out into the garden and you tread on a thorn, always remember to say thank you. The thorn may hurt, but it is given to you in the same way that you are given attar of roses."

I was too moved to say anything except to thank him. Dede went on, "The essence of the rose is released only when the rose bush has been pruned and pruned and the bud has opened into the bloom. He says to tell you that the split second between the bud and the rose is known only to those who become roses."

I left Dede's house the next day. It was better that I go quickly. Early in the morning we went to the mosque where Dede prayed, and then on to Mevlana's tomb for the last time. He was very quiet, deeply moved and sad, and our movements as we toured the museum took on a different meaning. As usual we walked out of the building backwards, bowing as we crossed the threshhold. Then, having collected our shoes and the suitcase that I had taken to the museum, he hailed a taxi and we drove to the bus station. Farid was there to see me off with a big basket of fruit in his hand, and Dede's wife arrived with a beautifully wrapped parcel of honey cakes and sugared almonds.

"Salaam aleikhum"—he called as I boarded the bus and waved to him from the top of the steps. He spoke to Farid, who added, "Don't forget—your home is here."

As the bus moved off Farid shouted, "Dede says, don't forget to take the rosewater to the West." And then we had turned the corner and were on the long road south.

eleven

The day is not far distant when humanity will realize that biologically it is faced with a choice between suicide and adoration.

—Pierre Teilhard de Chardin

God is never seen immaterially; and the vision of Him in woman is the most perfect of all.

—Muhyi-d-din Ibn Arabi

The Great Way is not difficult
for those who have no preferences.
When love and hate are both absent,
everything becomes clear and undisguised.

—Sengtsan, Hsin Hsin Ming

The weather had changed since the last time I had been in Sidé. The cold winds had passed, and already the sun was hot, bringing out the spring flowers in the fields and under the olive trees. The men were in the streets, painting the houses and the café, readying the town for the tourist season, while in the fields the women were bent over the long furrows, planting vegetables for the summer harvest. I had rented a Jeep for the drive from Antalya to Sidé, with quite a different sense of expectation than I had experienced before. When I had first come to Turkey I had been motivated by the anticipation of discovering the mysteries of the Dervishes, of powers that might be developed, and of a different way of life that could be lived with the knowledge that I had hoped to gain. The weeks of traveling, and the constant tests and disappointments, had finally brought me to face the knowledge that if I were to proceed any further on the path, all those ideas had to be given up. There is a mystery in the moment which can unfold only when all our hopes and fears have been surrendered. As the Jeep neared Sidé, along the dusty road past the amphitheater, I knew that this would be the last time, at least for a while, that Hamid and I would be working together. I did not know exactly what had happened, but I did know that something had changed so radically within me that it was time to leave Turkey and put what I had learned and experienced to the test of everyday life. My thoughts and feelings were still muddled, and there was much that could not be explained, but without hope or expectation I knew that when the time was right, I would begin to understand.

I was no longer afraid of Hamid. In fact I had not realized until then just how fearful of him I had been. After the first enthusiasm of my arrival in Turkey, my fear had grown until at times it verged on terror. Hamid was still an enigma to me; yet, despite the mystery of his strange behavior, I was convinced that what he was trying to pass on to me was correct, and of great importance. It was this conviction that had kept me going through the most difficult periods.

Dede, in his kindness and total acceptance of me, had helped me to surrender to what lay behind Hamid's words, behind his anger and apparent harshness. Dede had neither questioned nor criticized when I told him of my experiences with Hamid. He would just smile and nod as the translation was made, and say, "How wonderful are the ways of God, Who manifests for each of us all that is necessary for the moment."

Until my second trip to Konya, when I was received by Mevlana, I had been fighting the idea that there is an all-knowing Being or life-force to which we are eternally bound, and therefore there is some part of us that has always known the Truth and always will. Hamid had said to me in England,

"The Soul is a knowing substance. If you know who you are then you know what it is, and that substance permeates all life, but first you must find your soul, your essential self. You must discover who and what you are, and only then will you be at the threshhold of the Way." Expectation and hope had produced so many fears—the fear of failure, of failing to gain entrance into the Way. There was the fear of losing mind and health in the process, the fear of what it might mean to give up everything in order to come into the "real world."

Now that I had begun to learn about the arrogance of expectancy and hope, I realized that what I had to work on was not the heart, the seat of the soul, but on the endless layers of conditioned mind, and on the body, and on those energies that must be able to flow freely if we are to become balanced human beings.

Hamid came out of the house to greet me as I drove the Jeep up to the gate of the courtyard. His manner was casual, as though I had scarcely been away, but he seemed really glad to see me, and immediately went into the kitchen to prepare coffee. "Go out and sit in the sun," he said. "The spring flowers are just beginning to show themselves. I will be right out."

In the center of the patio stood a little table covered with a pile of Hamid's papers. I sat down on one of the white painted wooden chairs and looked up at my old room, and below at the girl's room. Her blinds were drawn, but I could sense her presence there. She was another mystery, one that I still longed to unravel.

Hamid seated himself beside me and poured the coffee. "Isn't it beautiful now that spring is coming. Spring is my favorite time in this part of Turkey, when the air is warm and the chill of winter is gone. Later, when it gets unbearably hot, I will go to Istanbul. The tourists come to Sidé, though; they seem to like lying out there on the beach as though they were pieces of driftwood, getting all burned and dried up. But that is their wish.

"But now you must tell me all about what you have been doing in Konya and what has transpired. I have been looking forward so much to your return. First of all, please tell me exactly what happened when you went to visit Shams–i Tabriz and Mevlana. Did you sit there for three days and three nights as you were instructed?"

I described my experiences at great length. He was particularly interested when I told him of the changes I had felt within myself at the moment I entered the tomb of Shams–i Tabriz. "When I walked in there, all I knew was the overwhelming presence of love. It wasn't like anything I'd ever experienced before—there was nothing I could do but let the power wash right through me. In fact, it was almost as though 'I' weren't there at all."

Hamid leaned back in his chair. All he said was, "Ah, Shams." We were silent for a time, and then he added, "May you never recover."

I went on to tell Hamid about my meeting with Dede, how he had taken me to his house, and that he had known the old man in Istanbul. I had wondered about the old man ever since the day when Hamid had taken me to see him, and now the time seemed right to ask about him.

"I wondered if you would finally ask that," Hamid said. "But it does not really matter. All that matters is that you were accepted by him, which showed me that, despite what you thought, and despite the difficult time that you had in the pension, you had been accepted to undertake the next stage. Even if I told you his name, would you really know any more about him? Let us just say that he is a man of great knowledge. He was happy for you, happy to be able to send you once more to Mevlana. He knew that your intention and your motive were becoming free at last of any ambition, or of any preconceived ideas of what this visit might entail. If your motive had not been clear, you would not have met Dede, who was able to provide you with the rest and comfort that you so badly needed. He would not have come if you had not been accepted by Mevlana, for Dede's love of Mevlana enabled him to know exactly where you stood and whether you were to be allowed to start the next stage of your journey.

"Now you are at the real beginning. I am sorry that it has been such a hard time for you. It was not my wish, but you came to me with so many ideas of what this path is about, and what you thought you wanted, and what you thought would be useful for you, that it was really impossible for me to do anything except to set up the best possible circumstances for you to do what you had to do. Because you really did want to know, it was possible for various scenes to be set up in which you played a part, learning a little more each time.

"We have much more to talk about today. First, though, let's make some more coffee and get some food together. You must be hungry after your trip."

We both laughed when he produced a jar of black olives, flavored with mint and lemon. "These have been waiting for you," he said. "I got them ready when you first came to me, and then screwed the lid on tight. They should be just about perfect." He gave me a wink and spooned some out onto my plate. We ate them with rough bread and cheese, and a salad made of lettuce and tomatoes flavored with dill weed.

When we had finished eating, I asked the question that was uppermost in my mind at the moment. "Hamid—is the girl still here?" He looked up sharply, and for a moment I thought he was going to get angry again. "Yes, she is here. She is in her room."

"She's had a tremendous impact on me, even though I've seen very little of her. I've never met anyone like her—she's a complete mystery to me."

"When you first came here," he said finally, "I did not want your attention to be deviated; but now it is time for us to talk, and to tie up all the loose ends of our time together.

"I'm sure you have realized that we have come to the end of this stage of our journey together. Tomorrow you will go back to England. Don't be sad or afraid—there's no reason for that."

I could not respond immediately. Even though I had

guessed that I would soon be leaving Turkey, Hamid's words came as a great shock. I felt suddenly that I could not bear to be separated from him. As usual he seemed to read my thoughts.

"Come now," he said. "Have you forgotten that He for Whom you are seeking is not to be found in the world of form? Until you can remember that, you will always be disappointed." He smiled gently, leaning back in his chair.

"You were asking me about the girl. She was sent to me to see if I could do anything to help her. She has been very ill, as you have seen, and for a long time she has been obsessed with that ball of wool. The doctors in England have not been able to help her. I will tell you her story—but I hope you will remember to look for the true meaning that lies below the surface of things. She has been damaged by going too far, without the proper training. In her yearning to be recognized, and thus to be freed, she went to different teachers in many countries around the world until, in her eagerness, she lost touch with her essential self, and has not yet been able to find the path again. You might say that she tried to surrender something that she had not yet found.

"There are three stages in the unfoldment of Truth. The first is made possible only through recognition, the recognition of our essential Unity with God. We have always been one with Him; but what we yearn for, deep in our hearts, is the actual knowledge of this fact. It is not enough to think that we know, for that is only a concept, not knowledge in essence. Recognition means coming, once again, into that state of gnosis from which we have been separated.

"When the girl comes to you with the wool wrapped round her wrists, like an imprisoned animal, she is begging you to see her, begging you to understand and to free her through recognition and understanding. Yet, until you discover your true self, how can it be possible to recognize another?

"It is almost as though the girl has been sent to us as a messenger, a continuous reminder of our responsibility in being born man and woman—the responsibility of finding our true self so that we may play our part in bringing others into that great freedom. That is the second stage, which is redemption. The third stage is what is sometimes called resurrection. But it will take more time in our world before you are ready to understand.

"I think the girl is recovering now. We will see her later on, and you may notice a change. I have been working with her to help her re-form the matrix of her true self. I have been in touch with some friends of hers who will shortly be coming here to take her back to England. They also plan to stay with me for a while to study."

Hamid leaned back in his chair and closed his eyes. This action had become a signal for me to be as open as I could, to try to understand the things that he had been speaking of. During moments like this, it seemed as though I were being lifted into another dimension of understanding, where the rational mind was still and some other faculty, for which I had no words, was allowed to become active. As I listened to Hamid's words, I knew that the girl with her ball of blue wool was not just another sad creature, unable to care for herself, but that she and her pain represented something far greater than I had yet been able to realize. I saw, for that instant, her place in my journey—and my place in hers. Each piece of the jigsaw puzzle had seemed complete in itself; now it was time to try to put the pieces together.

After an indefinite time I opened my eyes to find Hamid watching me. We sat quietly for a little longer, and then he said, "Our time together is very short now; there must be many questions that you want to ask."

In that instant I became aware of a feeling of great pain at the thought of parting from Hamid. At the same time I felt that I was actually experiencing the suffering of the girl. It seemed that there was only one question to be asked.

"Why does it all have to hurt so much?"

"Did I not tell you, 'I pity you?' When you truly say 'I will' unconditionally to a life of service to God, there is always pain and confusion at first. In the early stages you experience 'your' pain, or 'my' pain. But as we come to understand the nature of the path we have chosen we no longer see the pain as ours alone, but we begin to experience the suffering of a world ignorant of the Truth. This is the pain of separation, the cry of man wanting to know his essential unity with God. Yet this pain was never intended. God never wanted us to suffer, but if we are to come totally into knowledge, all illusion must be stripped away, leaving only clarity. It is our own arrogance and pride that cause the pain. The more we think that we can do anything, the less we realize our complete dependence on God, and the worse the pain becomes.

"And you, my friend, are particularly obstinate."

As he smiled at me I felt I understood the basic simplicity of life, and the complications that we create in running away from the essential self.

Hamid continued, "Finally there comes a time when you are so in love, so absorbed in the presence of God, that you welcome all that you are given, for you know that it comes from the One Source of All. With this different understanding, suffering becomes conscious. This conscious suffering is not the same as pain; nor does it mean enjoying pain, or believing that suffering must be good for you because it hurts. Conscious suffering comes about in the knowledge of what is necessary for the reciprocal maintenance of the planet. This earth was created for mankind, and we are responsible for it. The world needs certain kinds of food in the same way that we do. It needs the rain and the sun and the seasons so that it may bring forth fruit, and it needs other types of energy that mankind does not yet understand.

"Whenever anyone does come into true knowledge, a certain type of energy is released, made available for this great process of reciprocal maintenance. Normally this energy is released in sufficient quantities only during moments of great crisis, and particularly at the moment of death. But now we have reached the point in the life of the planet when we must learn to die to ourselves each moment, to be reborn each moment, to live and die consciously, so that the earth may continue to evolve. I hope that someday you will come to understand what I am saying. Now, though, we must go on to other things.

"Do you understand why it is necessary for you to go back to England now?

"I think maybe it's time for me to go away and try to absorb some of what I've been given these past weeks. I feel that I just can't take in any more right now."

"That is one of the reasons," he replied, "but there is another reason as well. You see, there comes a stage on this path when it is necessary to make the sacrifice of dependence on the teacher. The job of the teacher is to lead you to turn, once and for all, to God from whom everything comes. The teacher you find on earth is just a manifestation of the One who teaches all. But if you become dependent on the form of life then there is no chance of true understanding. And because it has been necessary for you to go through such a tremendous amount in a very short time, there is the added danger that you might find yourself believing that you were dependent on me. That is a dangerous trap, because really I am not here at all. Never forget—there is only one Teacher!

"Because you gave me your trust, not yet believing in God, I was able, for a little while, to act as your guide. But now you must go on. Go back to England, assimilate all the knowledge that you have been given. Then, when you are quite sure that you are ready, it will be your turn to pass on what you have learned, to help spread the knowledge of Unity to the world. The great Sufi Shaikh Muhyi-d-din Ibn Arabi once said, "Listen to God and return to Him! And when you have heard what was revealed to me, then impress it upon your hearts, and when you have understood it, the unity of what I have written, dissect it into parts and put it together again. Then reveal it to those that thirst for it and withhold it not from them! That is the grace which you have received, therefore transmit it to others." That is why we say, 'Devotion to God is studying Him in every aspect; serving God is teaching what you know of Him to others.'

"Serving God—what more beautiful thing is there to do! The only real joy is to be a servant of God, and that means being awake all the time to the needs of the moment. If we are asleep then we will never know what is required of us. We cannot have any preconceived ideas of what service means. We never know, from one moment to the next, what will be asked of us. When you enter the path you put yourself in the stream of service for the rest of your life. There is no going back. Do not think that you can be of service only when you want to be of service! You must be awake to the needs of the moment, God's needs, not to your own needs. Only then may you be granted the privilage of being of service.

"It is said that there are only two things that God cannot give us, but that we must give to Him—servility and dependence. When we come to realize our complete dependence on God, beyond any concepts or expectation of reward, we are given exactly what we need to fulfill our task. It is also said that 'God has no needs—so give Him yours.'

"You have a special link with Mevlana; that is why you were sent to Konya, and why you were received as you were. It is from Konya that your journey begins.

"There is something that I want to try to explain to you now. Please listen carefully, and try to understand.

"Mevlana was a man who reached Union with God, and therefore there was no separation any more. Mevlana and He to Whom he surrendered were One. Many of those who follow the mystic path have a glimpse of what this could mean, but complete absorption, complete Union, is granted only to a very few. As Mevlana reached Union, not only was he absorbed completely in Divine Love, but also he absorbed all those who had gone before him. Do you understand what I am saying to you? If you were to come into Union now, at this moment, then everything that had ever been would be revealed to you, since all that has been is known to Him from the beginning. He is love, lover, and beloved. He is the teacher, the pupil, and that which is taught. There is only

Him to which everything returns. I pray that one day you will truly come to understand and so be able to pass on what you know to others."

I could see that Hamid was growing very tired, and it was impossible for me to absorb at once the immense amounts of knowledge and energy that he was imparting. And yet I knew that he wanted to pass on something more before I left the next day. Abruptly he switched the topic of conversation once again.

"You may feel that I'm rushing you, that you can't possibly grasp everything that I'm telling you now. But the situation is more urgent than you understand, and I don't know when we will have the chance to be together again. I have told you a little of the second cycle of mankind. I think you understand that we are at the end of one great cycle of history and are verging on the next. Since evolution does not proceed in a straight line or curve but goes through very definite cycles, it is possible to know, through understanding of the laws that govern our life here on earth, something of what we may expect. Just now, as the end of the old cycle approaches, more and more knowledge will be released so that it may be preserved and carried on into the next cycle. It is not chance that we met as we did and spent time together here, or that you were sent to Konya. The knowledge that you have been given must be carried on as the first cycle of man is fulfilled. I cannot say what this will mean, nor can any man. But it is those who have reached the knowledge of their essential unity with God who will forge the way and build a new world. Before this new world can be brought into being, however, it is said that there are to be two confrontations. The first confrontation will be between those who know and those who do not want to know, and the second between those who know and those who will have to know."

"Hamid, do you mean that there has to be some sort of war? It seems that half the world at least has no desire to know of these things."

"Look inside yourself. Is it not so that both of these confrontations must take place within? There is a part of you, as there is a part of everyone, that does not want to know, and there are parts that will simply have to know, when the time comes, so that there is no separation any longer.

"What appears to be outside of yourself is really inside yourself. There is nothing outside, and so the battle is first of all within your own being. As more and more people go through these two confrontations, it is likely that we will see the battle materialized in the outer world. I don't say that there will or will not be a war. But what I do say, beyond any doubt, is that the whole world will one day be raised to know of its complete dependence on God. The choice that each of us must make is to surrender to God now, today, each moment—not at some nebulous future time when we will no longer be granted the privilege of choosing. But one way or another a confrontation will take place.

"It may be possible, if enough spiritual work is done in time, for a major disaster to be avoided. I am not the judge. But the second cycle of mankind will come about and with it the reappearance of the Christ. Some think that he will come again in the form of a man, and some say not. This is not important. What is important for you to know is that we will meet in the knowledge of Unity. So whatever the Second Coming means, and however it happens, it can only come about through the inner, hidden knowledge that underlies all the great religions and which unites us all. The New Age does not mean the formation of any new religion. Far from it. There will be no need, anymore, for any form of religion. All that will have to go. When you come upon the essence, do you still want the form? When you have drunk of the water of life, do you still need the glass to contain it? It has fulfilled its purpose and thus something new can come about. All I can say is that what will come about will be like nothing that has ever been seen before—not like any of the great civilizations of the past. I am speaking of a completely new way of life, and it is those with knowledge of Unity who must forge the way now. It is those people who can make decisions stemming from real knowledge who will breathe life and order into the New Age.

"But enough for now. We will take a break and rest for a while. I have ordered a special dinner at the restaurant, as it is to be your last night here, and we can talk further after the meal. In the meantime, why don't you go down to the beach? The sand is warm, even though the sea is still cold, and I'm sure you could use a break."

He walked slowly toward the house, pausing for a moment to bend down and smell one of the flowers in the center of the patio. I felt very alone, and very sad. It seemed to me that the knowledge and experience that Hamid had given to me had been waiting for centuries, and that those who held it could be free only when they had passed it on. My fear of Hamid was gone, and I felt only a deep yearning to understand all that he was trying to teach me.

I recalled my time with him, trying to remember all the things that had been said and the events that had taken place. I saw the journey as a pattern, a spiral that carried one to the center, and then immediately started out again toward the periphery. On the way occurred certain shock points which made it possible to procced to the next stage. When the center itself was reached, concepts no longer remained and there was only the necessity to face outward and to travel back again toward the place from which one had come. That place beyond all form, beyond all dogma and religious bigotry, beyond any concept of the mind, was represented to me by Mevlana Jelalu'ddin Rumi, for it was the experience of absolute Love itself that removed all the concepts and the outer form. Of one thing I was certain: if we are to help one another we must know who we are, and to know who we are it is necessary that we love God more than anything else so that, finally, there is only Him. Only thus can we truly be of service.

Just as the sun was going down I walked back along the beach. Tomorrow I would have to face the journey to London and the cold rain of the British spring. In some ways I was afraid, for I was raw, like a newborn child, or like someone who has been burned, exposed to the elements, waiting for the new skin to grow. But it was a challenge, and I felt a strength growing within myself, a strength that would see me through the inevitable changes that would result from my desire to bring what I had learned into a more normal style of life.

As I came up the path from the beach I saw that there was a strange car, a mini bus, parked outside the house. I had been so used to being alone with Hamid that my immediate reaction to the presence of other people was one of jealous anger. Stopping for a moment to get myself together, I realized that this bus probably belonged to the people that Hamid had mentioned, who were coming to study with him. Why was I so possessive? Did I not want the knowledge that he had given me to be passed on to as many others as possible?

I knew then that the battle with all that stands between us and the truth is constant, and that every day of our lives we must fight all that leads to separation.

"So there you are!" Hamid greeted me jovially as I entered the room. "We have a surprise—these are the people I told you about. They have driven all the way from India through Afghanistan and it took them a little less time than they thought, so here they are. Come, you must meet them."

I was taken round and introduced. There were five of them, two men and three women. One of the men had known the girl in London, and had kept in touch with her when she had come to stay with Hamid.

"I've just been telling them about you and some of the things that you have been doing. They seem quite concerned." Hamid leaned back in his chair, laughing. Gone was the urgency of the morning and of the things that he had been trying to convey to me. He was his old self, the Hamid I had known in London. Silently I asked him for help; for the shock of meeting all these people, and the fact that there were so few hours left and so much to be said was almost too much to bear.

As though in answer to my unspoken plea, he said, "So here we are. What a thing! But the good Lord knows best, and so it seems that we are to have a celebration tonight."

He pointed to me with a twinkle in his eye. "He is to go home tomorrow, and you are to start on the journey. And so it goes. One comes and goes and another comes. And then he goes. Yet it is He, the One God, who is coming and going at the same time.

"Now we must make arrangements for where you are all going to sleep, and then we must get ready for dinner. I will send a message to the restaurant that now we will be eight for dinner and not just three. Ah, they will be so pleased!"

When we all met again for dinner, I heard about the adventures of their trip through India and Afghanistan. But I found it impossible to tell them of my own experiences. We had all arrived at a new beginning, but I was returning to England, and they were staying in Turkey. They were so fresh and so eager, just as I had been. They felt that there was something to be learned from the Dervishes, or from Hamid, and although their reasons were different, I could see that their ideas of what they would find were similar to what mine had been. I found myself very quiet, almost unable to talk. I realized that these people had not yet learned to ask questions, and without a question there can be no answer. Remembering Hamid's lesson, I tried to allow the moment to unfold in front of me, without the need to project concepts and opinions as to what that moment might be. Everything was just exactly as it was, and it was just as it should be. When Hamid appeared, bringing the girl with him, the picture was complete. This evening she was neatly dressed, her hair was combed, and something had changed in her eyes. The desperation was gone. And more—the blue wool was no longer tangled around her wrists, but neatly wrapped into a ball, which she carried in her left hand.

She shook hands with everyone and then Hamid led her over to me. "Well," he said, looking at us both. She stopped in front of me, and there was a faint smile on her lips. "Well?" he repeated. She hesitated, looking to Hamid for help, but he just stood there, holding her arm, smiling. There was complete silence in the room, and a tremendous tension held us. Slowly she moved away from Hamid and took a step toward me, so that there was almost no distance between us. Her breath was hurried, and I felt that she was about to cry out. Without taking her eyes from mine, she stretched out her hand and gave me the ball of wool.

Hamid took us in his arms; both of us were crying with relief. Finally he took the girl by the hand and led her over to the group that had just come. "Look after her well," he said. Then he turned, laughing. "Come," he said, "dinner is waiting."

We ate well that night, fresh sardines broiled on wooden spits over a charcoal fire, and octopus marinated in olive oil. There were little meat balls, spicy and hot on the tongue, stuffed aubergine and tomatoes, and rice cooked with nuts and herbs. For the main course Hamid had ordered a huge fish that had been caught the night before. It was served to us on a platter, the skin crisp and basted with butter and fresh rosemary and decorated with wedges of lemon and cucumber.

The first fishermen were lighting the lamps of their boats for the night's work. The light caught the meshes of the nets, spread out on the tiny decks. Some of the men were singing as they prepared to set sail. The sky was filled with stars.

"Now," Hamid said, looking at me, "you have a task to do. Tell these people about this pilgrimage you have made, and something of what you have learned. Surely you know by now that life is really quite ordinary."

I don't know exactly what I said to them, but I remember that I spoke of service, and of the real world—the world of order, of pure light, the world that waits, and longs to be manifested in this relative world, but which can only come about when we, as conscious human beings, wake to know Reality. I think I talked about giving up all notions of what the path is about, and all ideas of what it is we think we want. I talked about zikr and remembrance of God. I talked about Dede, and how I had come finally to Mevlana, yet I think it was not what I said but what I felt and what I experienced as I spoke that moved them. "The language of the heart," I said to them, "is the language of love."

Then, just as I was getting almost too intense, the Gypsies arrived. I believe I was about to go deeply into the idea of recognition when I was interrupted by a pistol shot, followed by a lot of shouting. Into the square came a group of about ten Gypsies. One of them had a small pistol which he was firing in the air, others were beating tambourines, and one was tuning up a fiddle.

The owner of the café ran forward. He shouted over his shoulder, beckoning to us. I sat opposite Hamid and the girl. He looked at me kindly, and I felt then the same love that I had felt in Konya. The others had cleared a space between the tables and were dancing to the music of the Gypsies.

"So now we dance," Hamid said. "Tomorrow you will go, but before you do we will sit together. There is one more barrier that we have to cross. It is the last barrier before you can be freed into a new way of life. But now we dance. . . ."

"One last thing, Hamid," I said. "About the business with the egg in London."

"What about it?" he asked innocently, watching the dancing.

"Well, since you said that we must not get attached to phenomena, and that such things are not necessary, why did you break an egg on that man's head?"

He turned to me. "That particular detail was not only for the benefit of the sick man," he said. "That was for you as well. Remember—I know what attracts them."

epilogue

Reason is powerless in the expression of Love. Love alone is capable of revealing the truth of Love and being a Lover. The way of our prophets is the way of Truth. If you want to live, die in Love; die in Love if you want to remain alive.

—Mevlana Jelalu'ddin Rumi

When he has renounced the world so that he does not take to it on account of his (own) desire nor in compliance with the urges of his own self but just to fulfill the commandment of God, he is then commanded to talk to the world and establish contact with it because now there is a portion for him in it which cannot be discarded and which has not been created for any other person.

—Abdul Qadir Gilani

Hamid instructed me to sit under an olive tree, beside an ancient dry river bed that led down to the sea. It had been hot all day, and we had spent the early morning sitting together on the patio before going down to the beach. Now the afternoon breeze had come up, rustling the dry leaves, moving the brown dust in little spirals around my feet. The cicadas sang, a continuous whirr that made me think of the hills above Ephesus. I could sense where the sea washed up into the cove by the bend in the river bed. That was where she would be now, lying out in the sun with the others. Hamid and I had walked here from the beach to spend our last time alone together before my return to London. We had spoken little, content with the dry lazy sounds of the afternoon. Finally he turned to me.

"There is one more lesson I wish to pass on to you," he said. In some ways it is the most important of all, but if you did not already know what I am going to tell you, then you would not be able to hear what I have to say."

Abruptly his manner changed; once again he became the teacher, and I the pupil. "Sit up straight," he commanded. Your back must be straight so that the energy can flow freely. Without a good flow your understanding will be only partial. Words by themselves are just veils over the truth. If you are not awake, all you will have done is to separate yourself again. Understanding does not come from the senses; understanding comes from itself. It is the overflowing of knowledge which is given as an act of grace for which we must prepare.

"Today we are going together to meet the Perfect Man, the Master who has come to love God so perfectly that God's attributes pour out through him into the world with no veil between. So far, in our talks and practices, we have been involved only with the work that it is necessary to do on oneself to prepare for the journey. Today you will have a taste of the work to come.

"Be very still, your back straight, your breathing relaxed. Choose the finest quality of air you can in the space around you. Draw it deep inside yourself, hold it for a moment, and then let it radiate from the center as light. Now close your eyes and withdraw your senses from the outer world. . . .

"The initiation you are going to take is dangerous. There are many pitfalls on the way and you must trust me absolutely. If you do not trust, if you lose courage, then I cannot help you and we may both fail to reach our destination. It is extremely important that you listen to my words and do what I tell you immediately. Don't hesitate, don't falter; and remember—trust!"

How many times had he said that to me? Once I had

thought that I knew what trust was, but then the tests began and I knew the meaning of failure, failure to trust, again and again. It needs so much surrender, and so much courage to be able to trust absolutely. . . .

"I want you to imagine that you are walking along a path in a valley; in front of you is a mountain. Near the summit, sitting outside a cave, the Perfect Master awaits you. You are walking up the path, aware with every step to the earth under your feet. The earth is warm; take off your shoes so you can feel it more easily. Be aware of the deep grass on either side of you . . . can you see the butterflies feeding on the nectar of the wild flowers? And hear the insects? Observe carefully—what do you notice as you walk? Now you see that the path starts to ascend the mountain. It is a steep path, but you must leave the valley behind and start to climb."

I became aware of the change as I left the valley behind. The feeling was different. All around me pine trees pointed to the sky, each one trying to reach the light. It was dark in the forest, no sun filtered through the trees. The windsong of the branches was the only sound. For a moment there was fear, and then I heard Hamid's voice once more.

"Keep walking—you have a long way to go. Do not turn back now."

I walked on up the path. After a little while I heard the sound of water to my left. Turning in that direction, I came upon a series of waterfalls cascading over enormous gray stones. At the bottom a deep whirlpool was formed, a rushing spiral that drew everything into itself and then spun it out in brilliant streams that rushed in and out of the rocks, forming more eddies and whirlpools. I sat and rested for a moment, watching and listening. Suddenly I became aware that the water was alive! Each bubble in the foam released a subtle form as it burst, each stream and eddy called out, "Look, do you see who I am? Can you hear my voices?" I saw that the water was observing me. I was not looking at it, but rather as I realized that it could see me, I recognized what it was and what it was saying. I wondered how I could have spent my life looking at the elements, never allowing myself to be seen, never reversing the space.

Hamid spoke once again. "Be careful. What you see can lead you astray, for it will want to take you into itself. You have seen so that you may understand and eventually gain mastery of certain aspects of energy. That is all. Now breathe deeply; feel yourself purified by the elements of water. Be washed through, and let us go on."

For a moment my mind went back to the beach. The sound of the crashing water made me think of the surf in the bay. She would be lying there now, with her friends, her skin the color of the sand. Or perhaps she would be swimming, far out by the rocks.

I got up from where I had been sitting and walked on once again. The air was getting lighter and I could see patches of sunlight on the path and under some of the trees. There were fewer trees now; soon I would be above the timber line and onto the rock face.

"Good. You have seen the sun through the trees and flashing on the water. Now I want you to feel the sun on your chest as you leave the last of the trees behind. Feel the sun as though it were for the first time in your life—or the last. It is the early morning sun and it warms every part of you, spreading from the center of your chest through the veins, along your arms, down your legs and then up your back to your head so that your body is warmed through. This is the element of fire that burns out the dross to leave only pure light. Feel yourself purified with the fire of the sun."

As I relaxed into the warmth of the sunlight I realized that it, too, had an awareness, a voice that could be heard. It was different from that of the earth and the water, but it too spoke to me and led me to itself. Almost at once I heard sounds, voices calling out, "Why go on?" "What more do you want than this?" "We will become one again."

I could feel my whole body glow and a yearning surged through me that I had not known before, as though some great force had been awakened and was drawing me into itself. I felt Hamid tug at my sleeve. "Wake up! Come on. This is not what you came for. You were shown these elements only so that you might recognize them and gain mastery over these aspects of the natural world and yourself.

"Take my hand now, for there is farther to go." We moved on together. In the distance the voices still appealed to me, but their attraction lessened as my confidence began to return.

"We are coming upon the last of the elements, the element of air. You must be very careful, for this is the most powerful element of all. In ancient cultures this force was often revered as a god, with its own laws and initiations. You will face a test now, but I will be here as a guide. Remember to trust and you will be all right.

"Now imagine that you are an eagle, standing on that rock. Go on, walk to it. Now let all your limbs become loose like the eagle ruffling his feathers in the morning air. Spread your arms a little so that you can feel the wind between your arms and your body and let your legs be a little apart. Breathe the air. Breathe as you have never breathed before. Be breathed! Let the wind breathe you! Feel the wind blow through your body, between the muscles and the fibers, through the veins, between each atom. . . ."

I let myself relax and tried to imagine what it would be like to be an eagle on the rock. I felt a sense of power—perhaps I *could* soar on the wind! I felt the air pass through me, separating the atoms from the molecules, passing through the muscles and the fibers. No more was I breathing, I was being breathed! At the same time I felt a wave of dizziness and I became aware that something was trying to draw me off the mountain. I struggled to remain alert, but I could not stop myself from drifting off into a deep sleep. I could hear Hamid's voice from a great distance, but his words were carried away by the sounds of the air rushing through me. It would be so easy to let go now, to surrender to the wind. It was fine, so easy. I had always wanted to fly into space, away from the earth and the oceans, soaring to catch the thermals, higher and higher in the wind. There was no need to go farther. . . .

I was jarred at that moment by garbled shouting, many voices at once; and someone was shaking me. "You must not go to sleep. You must stay awake. Wake up! Wake up! The wind is trying to draw you off the rock face. You did not come so far to sleep now. Wake up!"

With every bit of strength I had left I struggled to wake. The wind still roared through me, but little by little I could again see what was around me. "Trust—hold on with everything you've got. Show this element that you acknowledge it but that one day you will be its master. Then the winds will be your friend."

I stepped down off the rock, onto the path. "You have now passed through the elements; from here, you are to go on alone. Ahead of you, above that rock, is the one you have traveled so far to meet."

I had almost forgotten! The Master was there, the representative of Truth on earth. But what was that truth now? Nothing could be more beautiful, more powerful than the elements of the air and fire, the forces of the water and the earth. "Go on, go on. I have been there; now my job is to lead others who have been prepared as you have been. Go in awareness and in humility. He is waiting for you. When you find him, you are to sit about eight feet in front of him. I will remain here, but when you reach him you will hear my voice giving you instructions. Do what I tell you and do not be afraid."

Then he stopped and I went on alone. The last part of the climb was steep and difficult, and I felt fear; not the fear of death any more, not even the fear of failure, but the fear of that which lies beyond all phenomena, beyond all time and space.

I climbed around the rock. My foot slipped and I used my hands to lever my body over the last few yards. The noise of my feet on the rock was the only sound. My mouth was dry. On the other side of the rock was a narrow crevice through which I must climb. I tried to be awake in every atom of my being, for I knew that he was there. Using my hands on the steep rock face and bracing my shoulders against the rock on either side I pulled myself through.

I was in his presence! For a moment I was too afraid to go forward and I could not look at him. But I could hear Hamid's voice. "Go on. Do as I told you. Seat yourself about eight feet in front of him. It is all right."

I sat down, and for a long time I could not raise my eyes. Tears poured down my face; not bitter tears, or tears of grief, but tears of absolute joy and thankfulness. I looked up. I seemed to be looking at one face that was many faces; everything whirled around it, but the face itself was still. The smile he gave me removed my fear; all that remained was that one moment in which was contained everything that had been, and everything that would ever be.

"Feel the perfect love that pours from Our Master into you, the love that shatters all illusion, love that has no conditions attached to it, love that heals and redeems. There is only the Master and you and that Absolute Love manifesting through him to fill every part of you."

I felt my heart open to his words. I had not known before that love has a sound, but it was the sound of love that seemed to shatter me. It was like no sound on earth and yet it contained all sound. Nothing could withstand the power of it; every part of my being vibrated, resonating to the sound that revolved and spun out from the center. Everything was sound, spinning and circling, moving the planets in their orbits, permeating every molecule and atom. What I thought I was died in it, was drowned in it, was redeemed through it back to the source of life.

Then I heard the voice of Hamid once again. "Do not go to sleep, whatever you do. You must be more awake than ever before. You have been allowed to feel the timeless presence of love. Now feel the light of God pouring from the Master into you."

Slowly the sound cleared, and I began to feel a glow of pure light proceeding from him into me, penetrating my being, growing in intensity. It came to me first as colors, myriads of sparkling colors within that one light, like fireflies by the ocean. Each one flew to me, burst inside me, blinded me. It was so beautiful that I was captured by it.

"Do not avert your face!" came the command. As I heard those words the colors became still more intense, and then, from the many colors, a perfect shade of blue illuminated everything. It was as though he had become the instrument for a blue light so intense that it blotted out every other color. Gone were the golds of the sun and the yellows and pinks of dawn, the rich reds, mauves, and greens. There was only limitless blue.

I remembered the words, "Do not avert your face," and from somewhere came the thought that, if one were brave enough and well enough prepared to die in life, then from the beauty of the colors would come the pure white light, the light that makes color visible. I had traveled for a long time and now I felt I could accept that light. There was nothing else that I wanted.

From the moment of recognition of that yearning a change began to occur. First the blue began to shimmer with silver streaks that sparkled with tremendous brilliance; and then, from within the blue itself, poured a blinding whiteness. It seemed to come from the center of all life. It was a light brighter than light, before all the light that can be seen in this world. I surrendered to it, opened myself to it, let it take from me the last shred of my past, purifying me, until there was nothing left of me.

Hamid's voice came to me from far away. "For anything to manifest in this world it is necessary that the Divine Power pierce the veils that separate us from the real world. Let this power fill you now."

I was very still, waiting, numbed by all that was happening to me. Then, seemingly far away at first, I heard a rumbling, like thunder in distant hills. The rumbling grew to a roar and I put my hands to my ears to blot out the sound. I realized then that the sound came also from within myself, that there was nothing I could do to escape it. I wanted silence more than anything in the world. I looked at the Master, pleading, but he was completely impassive and undisturbed; the power of the sound simply passed through him. I came to the point where I felt that I could not bear it any longer and then, through the roar, came Hamid's voice once again, steady and calm. "Do not be afraid," he said. "Few people are given this chance. You have only to surrender to the power that brings everything into being and you will be safe."

Again I opened, letting go of all resistance. From out of the sound grew a vision of worlds being born, of whole galactic systems bursting into life, of light crystalizing into form, and I heard a voice saying to me, "Know and understand. For every true act of surrender a man or woman makes a galactic system is born, and whenever a human being finds his true Self a universe bursts into life. Now that you have seen and been seen you may feel a peace that you have never known."

As the vision faded I felt I had known a glimpse of the understanding of perfection. It was possible to accept unconditionally what is, what has been, what will be. Everything was there. There was neither beginning nor end; the Creator and that which was created were one. Everything is in one moment. Everything is Him. That is the secret of predestination. Nothing has ever happened, for everything is already here.

The overwhelming presence radiated a peace that truly passed all understanding, and there was no more separation. He and I were as one and the peace that I felt from Him was within myself, in the realization of the Unity and Perfection of God. It seemed that there was nothing further to do. There was only to be.

For a long time I sat on the mountain facing him. In realization there is no time. The earth turned, the seasons came and went, men and women were born and died, worlds came into being, all passing through the space in which I sat. All the masters, saints, and prophets throughout time manifested on that stage and as they told their stories they were swept into the eternity of Being. In that perfect peace I realized that all the great teachers were coming out of that presence of Being and passing on their way, just as were the suns and the stars, the lightning and the rain and the children that were being born. Then I heard the voice of Hamid.

"It is time for you to open your eyes. But prepare yourself carefully, for what you see will shock you. This is the last test of this stage of our journey together—the last barrier that you must overcome.

"I want you to bring your consciousness slowly back to the world. Can you feel your body? Good. Now become aware of your breathing. Listen to the breath of your heart, feel the blood coursing through your veins. Move your fingers around a little. Feel you body. Smell the mountain air, taste the saliva in your mouth. . . ."

Suddenly I felt very confused. I was neither in the real world that I had been experiencing nor did I seem to be in the world that I had left in the valley. I could hear Hamid's voice, but in my bewilderment I did not know where it was coming from. I moved my fingers, and breathed deeply. I tried to become more and more aware of my body sitting there on the mountainside.

"Now, very slowly, open your eyes."

Suddenly I understood what it was to be completely alone. There was no one there!

I shut my eyes again and tried to understand. Was I dreaming? Where was I? Where was Hamid? Where was the Master, whom Hamid had called "Perfected Man?" I was completely alone, outside that cave on the mountainside.

There was no one there, not even a stone on which he had been sitting. In front of me was the cave. Behind me stretched the valley and the path that I had climbed to reach this place. I did not dare move my head for a moment; I could only try to sense with my eyes what was happening.

"Now turn around and face the valley. Go on! Turn now. Turn."

Slowly I turned back. "Look out there across the valley. That is your world. In the valley are all the people who are waiting to climb this mountain to know the Truth. And now you have one last task. As your act of dedication in this world you must finally surrender your own life to a life of service.

"There was no Master on the mountain. That was a play of imagination, and yet it is so—that until we come to love God perfectly we cannot know love. Love is brought to life within you as you surrender to God so that there is only Him, and thus the possibility of perfected man. All that you have ever needed to know is here, now, within you. As you die to yourself you are reborn in eternity in which everything that has ever been, or ever will be, is waiting to be released to bring life to dying mankind. This is a terrible freedom, but it is the only real freedom."

Once more I looked about me. There was no one there, no movement on the dust of the path, no stone upon which he had sat. I was alone.

I breathed slowly and silently, watching the rise and fall of my breath. My back was sore where it had rubbed against the rough bark of the olive tree. My legs were cramped and they had lost all feeling. I must have been sitting there a long time. The scene was changing. The valley that stretched out before me gave way to a dried up river bed winding its way down to the sea. Cicadas whirred in the olive grove and in the distance I thought I could hear the surf in the bay.

Then I felt a hand on my arm and I looked up at Hamid. His eyes were deep with love and confidence. He smiled. "Come, Reshad," he said, "we must go home. They will be waiting for us."